BIG-NOTE PIANO

THE GREAT BIG BOOK OF CHILDREN'S SONGS

ISBN 0-7935-3920-X

HAL•LEONARD®
CORPORATION
7777 W. BLUEMOUND RD. P.O. BOX 13819 MILWAUKEE, WI 53213

CONTENTS

A-HUNTING WE WILL GO

Traditional

ABC-DEF-GHI

Words by JOE RAPOSO and JON STONE
Music by JOE RAPOSO

6

ARE YOU SLEEPING

Traditional

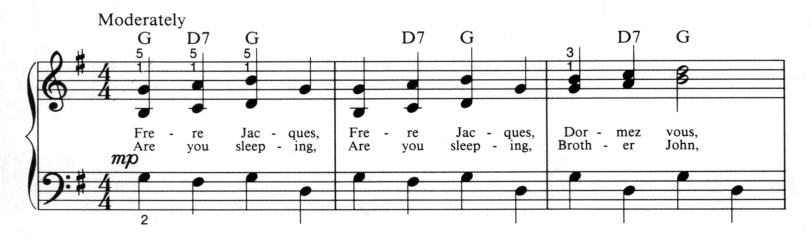

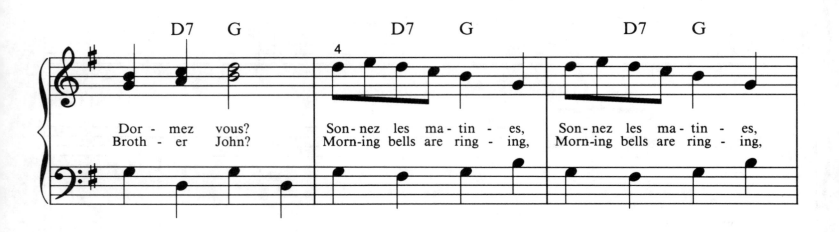

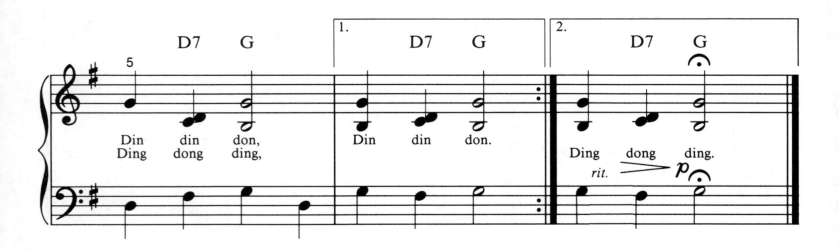

THE BARE NECESSITIES
from Walt Disney's THE JUNGLE BOOK

Words and Music by
TERRY GILKYSON

12

THE BALLAD OF DAVY CROCKETT

from Walt Disney's DAVY CROCKETT: KING OF THE WILD FRONTIER

Words by TOM BLACKBURN
Music by GEORGE BRUNS

King of the wild fron - tier!
man who — don't know fear!
-tier!

Additional Lyrics

3. Off through the woods
   he's a marchin' along,
   makin' up yarns
   an' singin' a song,
   itchin' fer fightin'
   an' rightin' a wrong

   He's ringy as a b'ar
   an' twict as strong

   Davy, Davy Crockett,
   the buck-skin buccaneer!

4. When he come home
   his politickin' done,
   The western march had just begun,
   So he packed his gear
   an' his trusty gun,
   An' lit out grinnin'
   to follow the sun.

   Davy, Davy Crockett,
   leadin' the pioneer!

5. His land is biggest
   an' his land is best,
   From grassy plains
   to the mountain crest,
   He's ahead of us
   all meetin' the test,
   Followin' his legend
   into the west.

   Davy, Davy Crockett,
   King of the wild frontier!

BE KIND TO YOUR PARENTS

from FANNY

Words and Music by
HAROLD ROME

18

BEIN' GREEN

Words and Music by
JOE RAPOSO

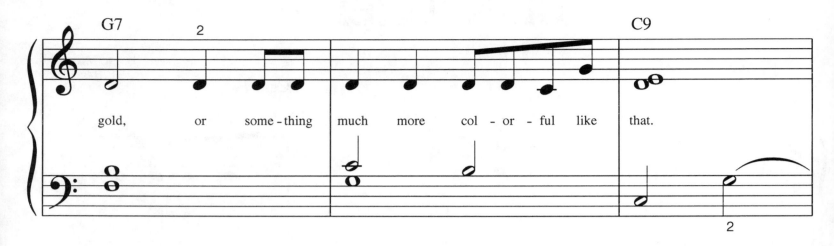

gold,   or   some-thing   much   more   col - or - ful   like   that.

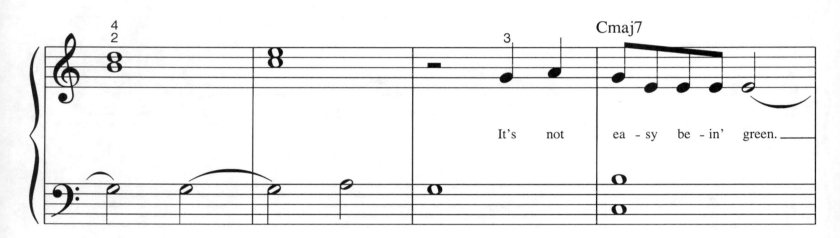

It's   not   ea - sy   be - in'   green. __

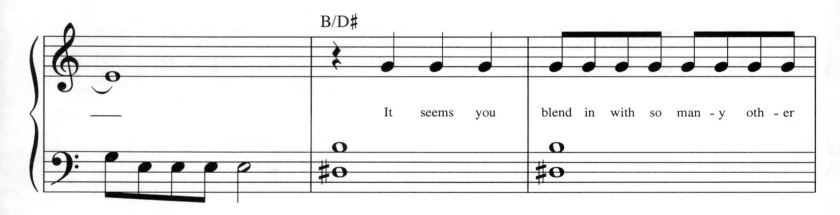

__   It   seems   you   blend   in   with   so   man - y   oth - er

or - di - na - ry   things, _____ and   peo - ple

Dm7

tend to pass you o - ver 'cause you're not stand - ing out like flash - y

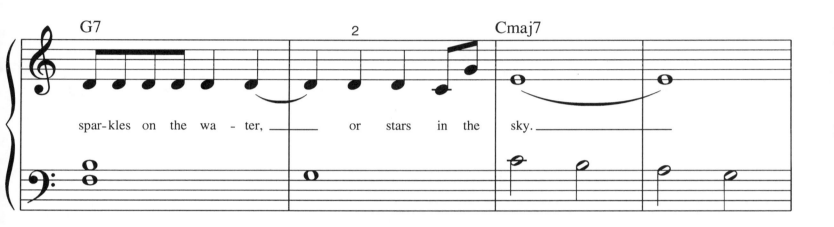

G7   2   Cmaj7

spar-kles on the wa - ter, _____ or stars in the sky. _____

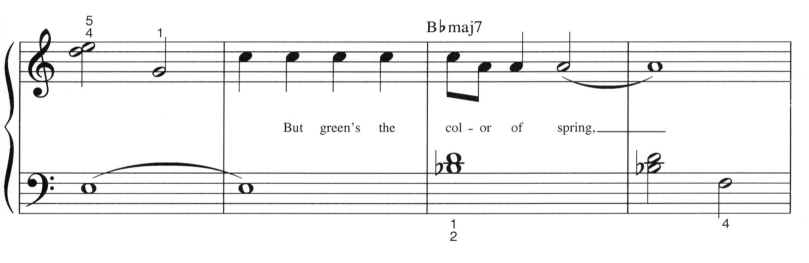

B♭maj7

But green's the col - or of spring, _____

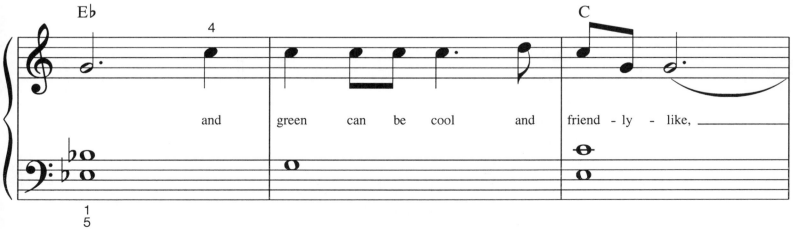

E♭   C

and green can be cool and friend - ly - like, _____

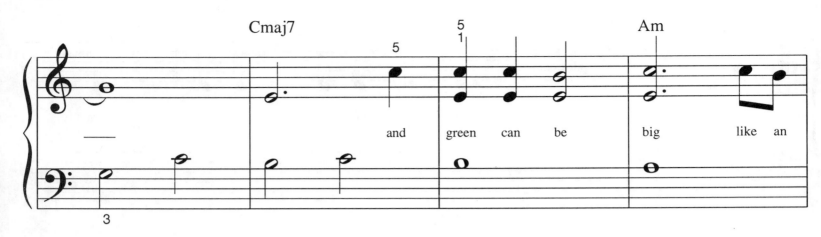

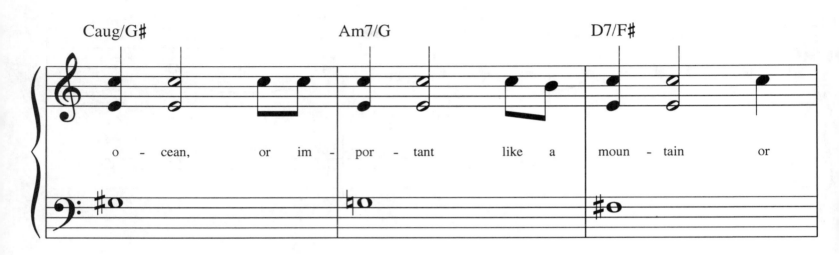

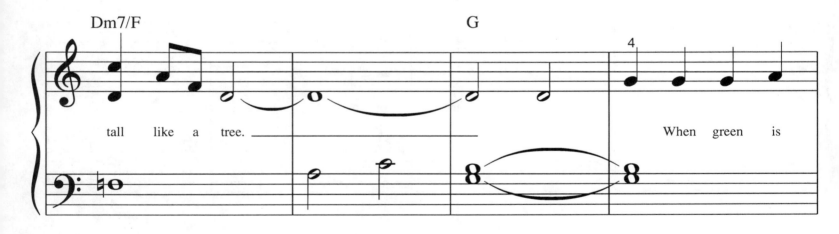

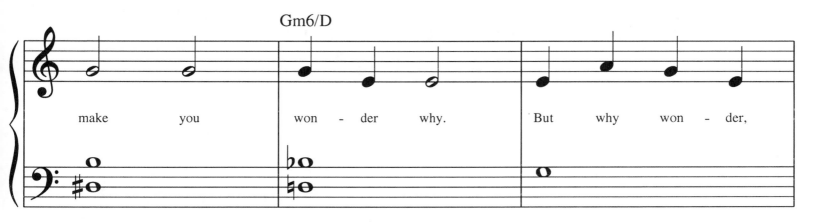

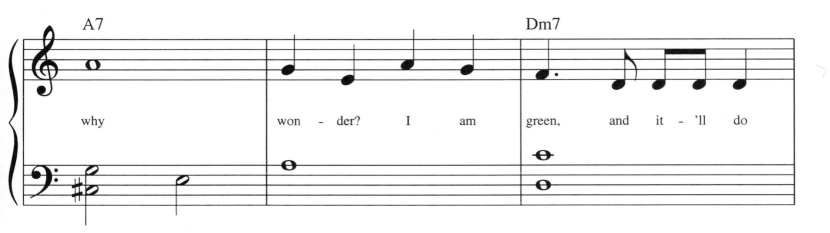

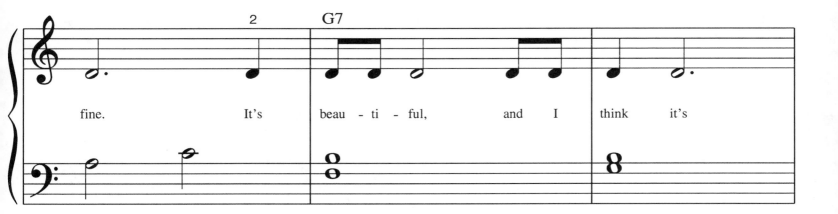

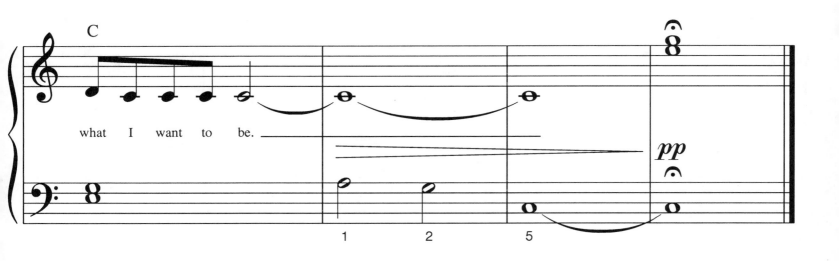

BEAUTY AND THE BEAST
from Walt Disney's BEAUTY AND THE BEAST

Lyrics by HOWARD ASHMAN
Music by ALAN MENKEN

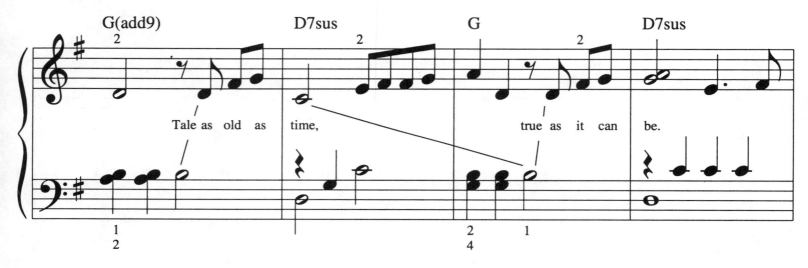

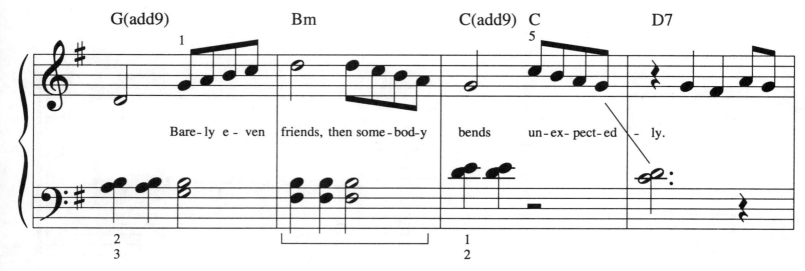

25

27

A BICYCLE BUILT FOR TWO
(a/k/a Daisy Bell)

Words and Music by
HARRY DACRE

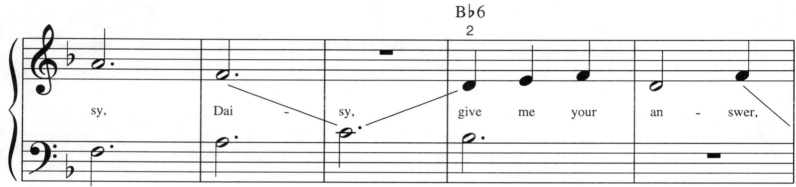

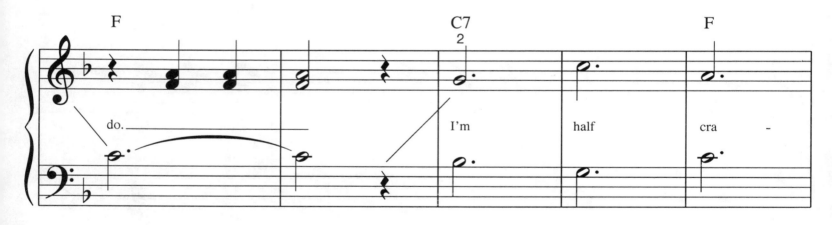

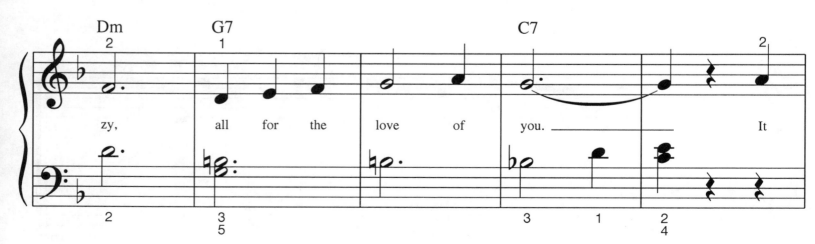

THE BRADY BUNCH
Theme from the Paramount Television Series THE BRADY BUNCH

Words and Music by SHERWOOD SCHWARTZ
and FRANK DEVOL

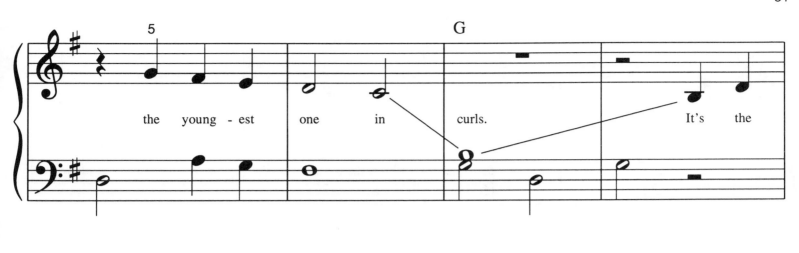

the young - est one in curls. It's the

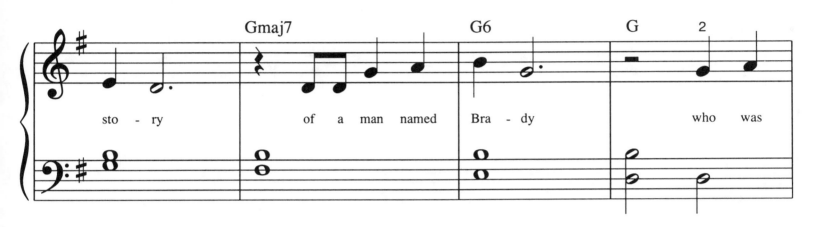

sto - ry of a man named Bra - dy who was

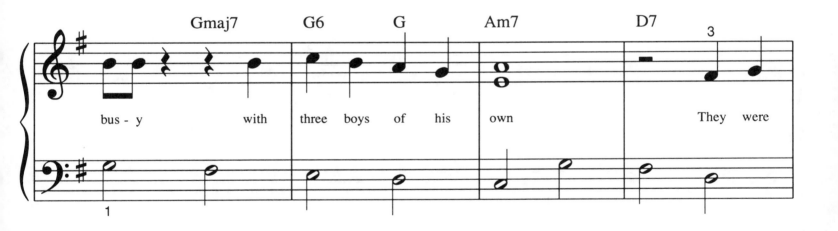

bus - y with three boys of his own They were

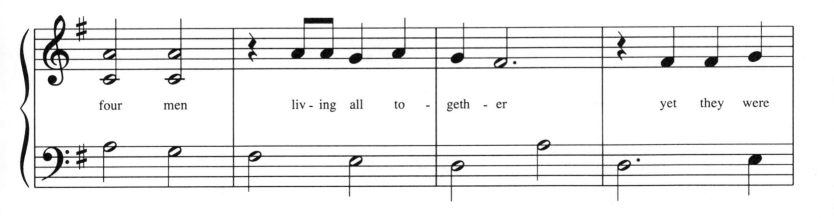

four men liv - ing all to - geth - er yet they were

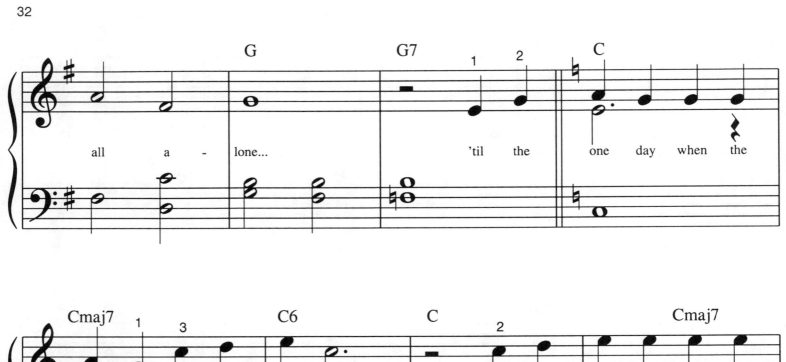

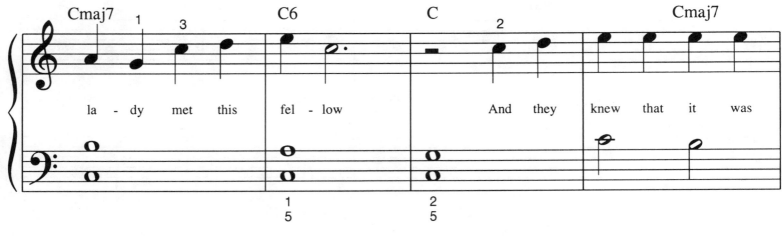

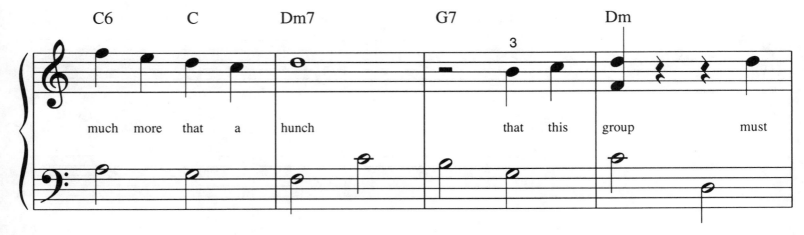

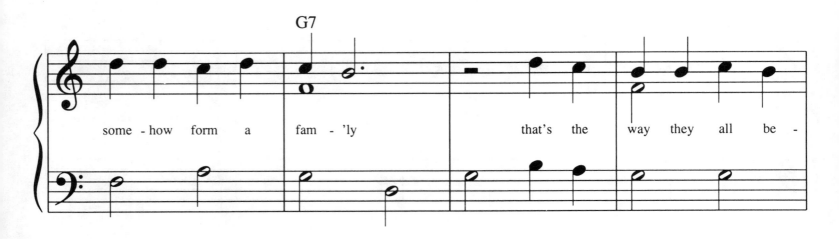

BUFFALO GALS
(Won't You Come Out Tonight?)

Words and Music by
COOL WHITE (JOHN HODGES)

Chorus

Buf - fa - lo gals, won't you come out to - night, come out to - night,

come out to -night? Buf - fa - lo gals, won't you come out to - night and

dance by the light of the moon? | 1.,2. | 3. moon?

2. I
3. I

Additional Lyrics

2. I asked her if she'd stop and talk, stop and talk, stop and talk,
   Her feet took up the whole sidewalk, and left no room for me.
   Chorus

3. I asked her if she'd be my wife, be my wife, be my wife,
   Then I'd be happy all my life, if she'd marry me.
   Chorus

THE BIBLE TELLS ME SO

Words and Music by
DALE EVANS

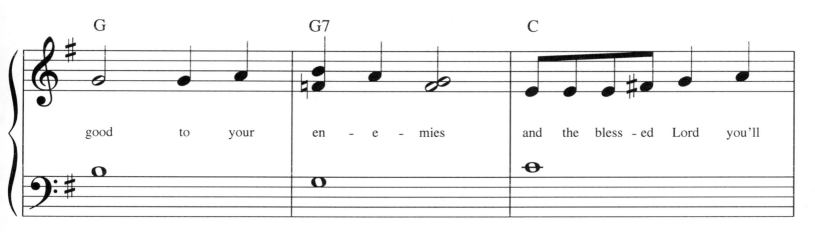

good to your en - e - mies and the bless - ed Lord you'll

sure - ly please. How do I know? The Bi - ble tells me

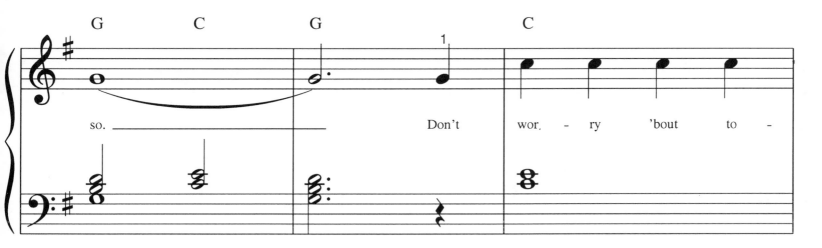

so. Don't wor - ry 'bout to -

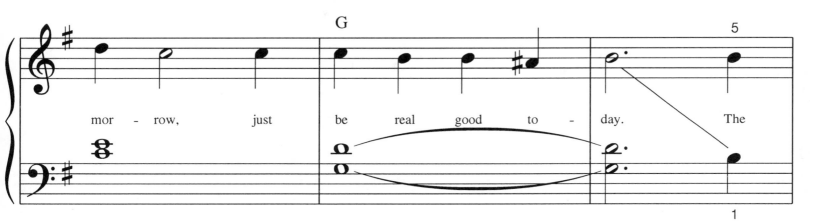

mor - row, just be real good to - day. The

CASPER THE FRIENDLY GHOST

from the Paramount Cartoon

Words by MACK DAVID
Music by JERRY LIVINGSTON

With spirit

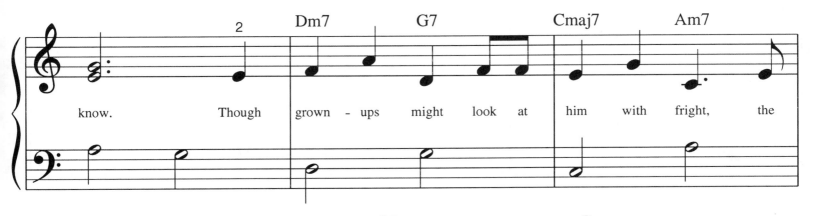

Cas - per the friend - ly ghost, the friend - li - est ghost you know. Though grown - ups might look at him with fright, the

chil - dren all love him so. Cas - per the

40

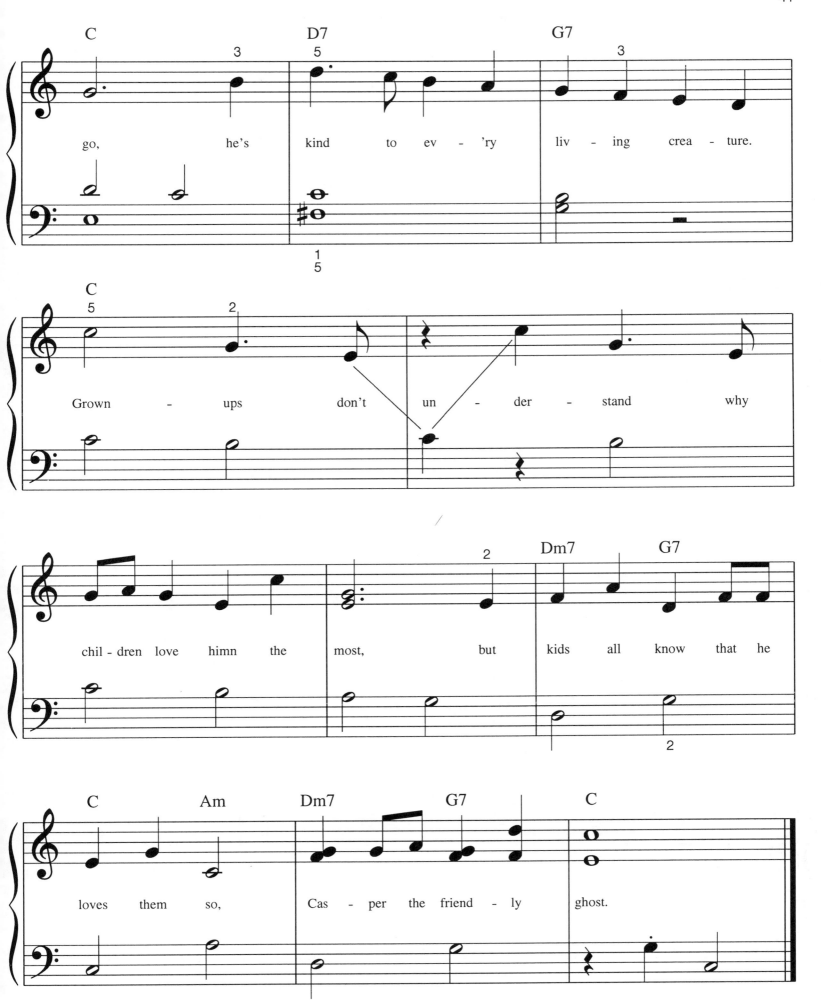

"C" IS FOR COOKIE

Words and Music by
JOE RAPOSO

THE CANDY MAN

from WILLY WONKA AND THE CHOCOLATE FACTORY

Words and Music by LESLIE BRICUSSE
and ANTHONY NEWLEY

45

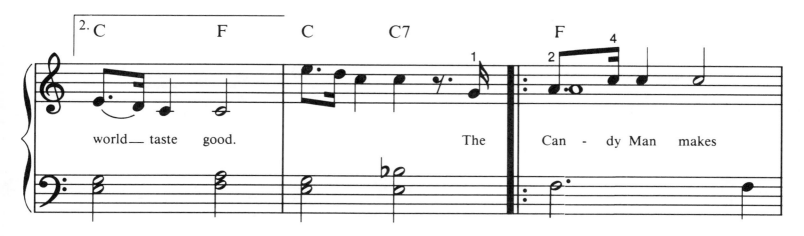

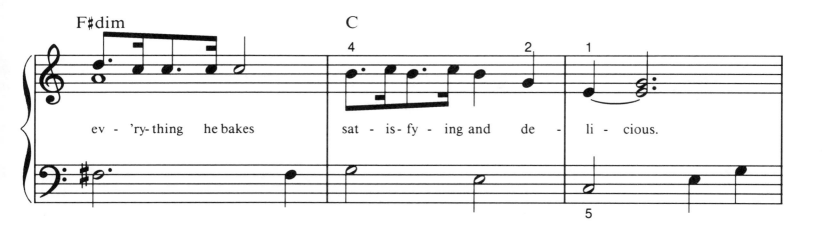

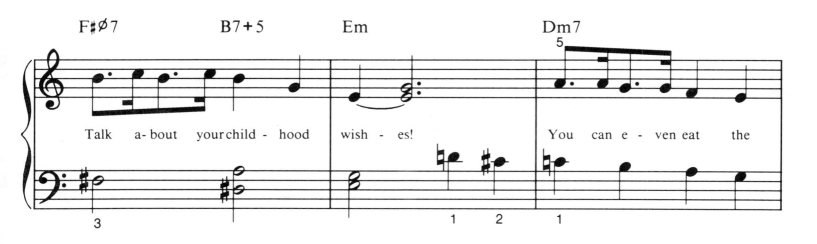

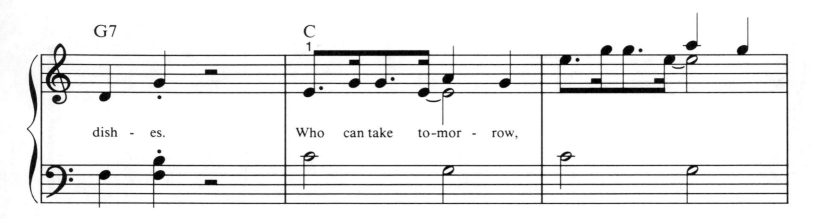

dish - es. Who can take to-mor - row,

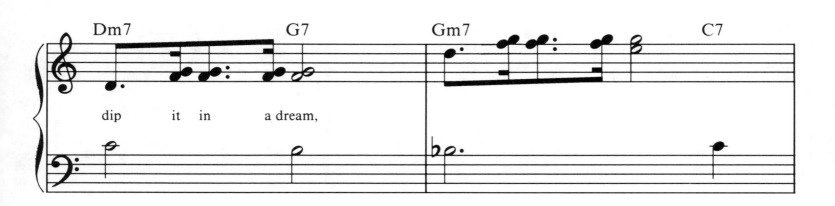

dip it in a dream,

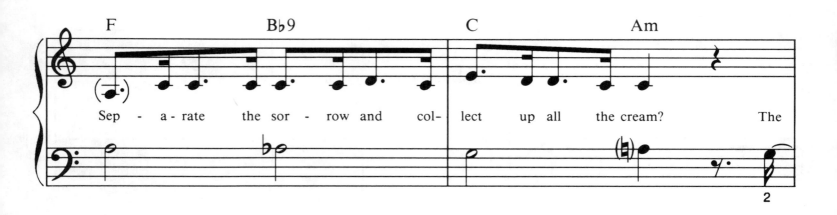

Sep - a - rate the sor - row and col- lect up all the cream? The

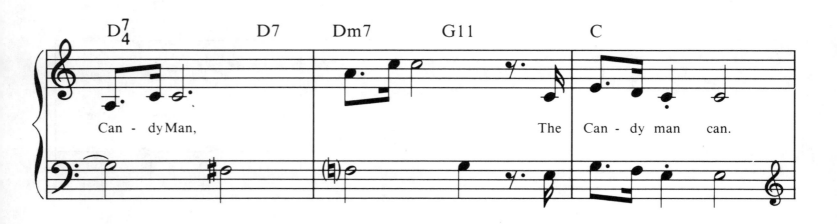

Can - dy Man, The Can - dy man can.

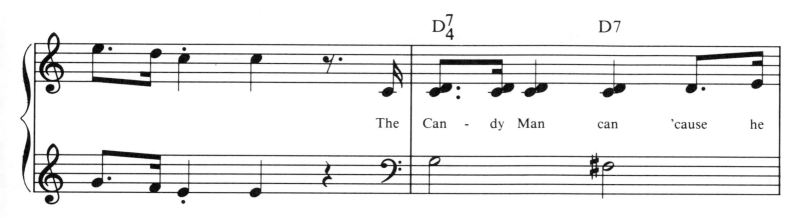

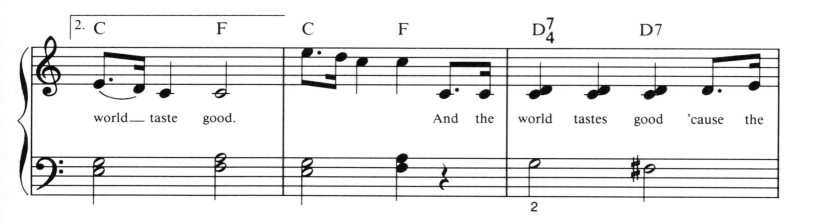

Repeat and Fade

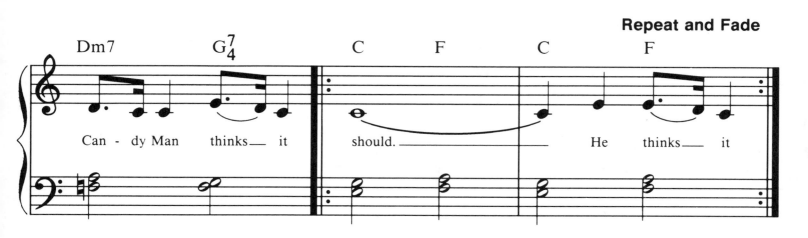

CIRCLE OF LIFE
from Walt Disney Pictures' THE LION KING

Music by ELTON JOHN
Lyrics by TIM RICE

Moderately, with an African beat

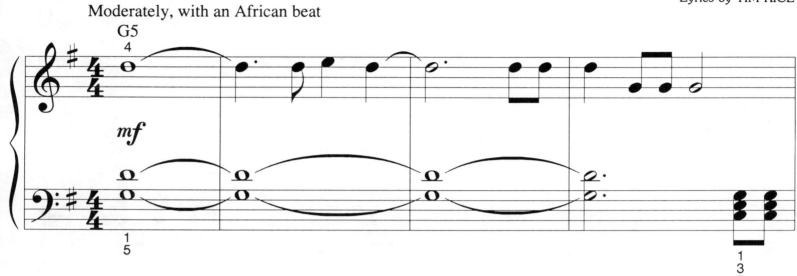

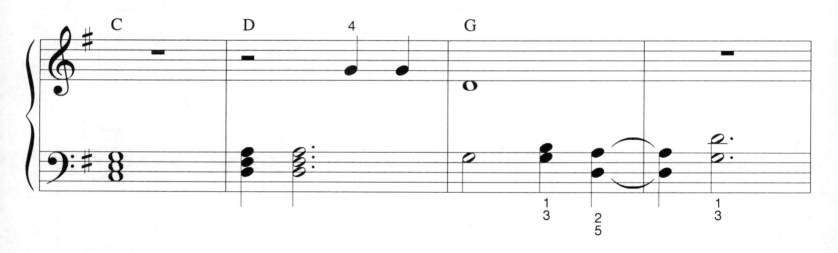

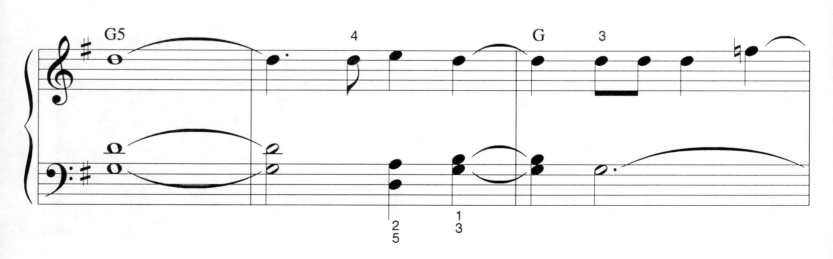

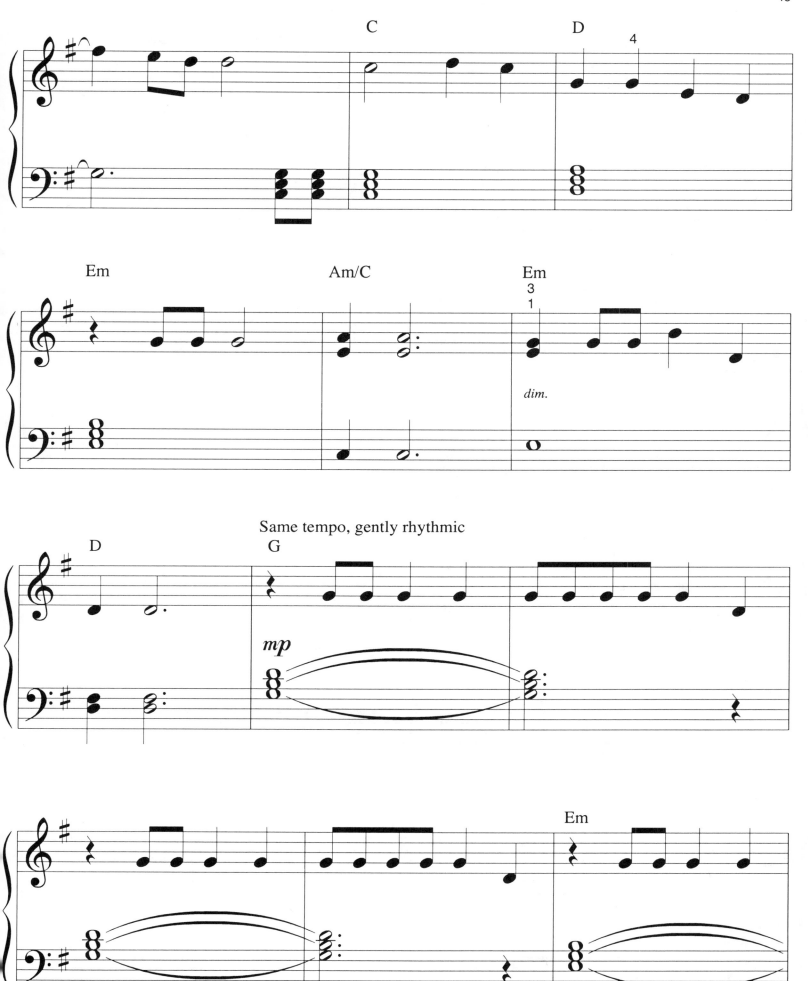

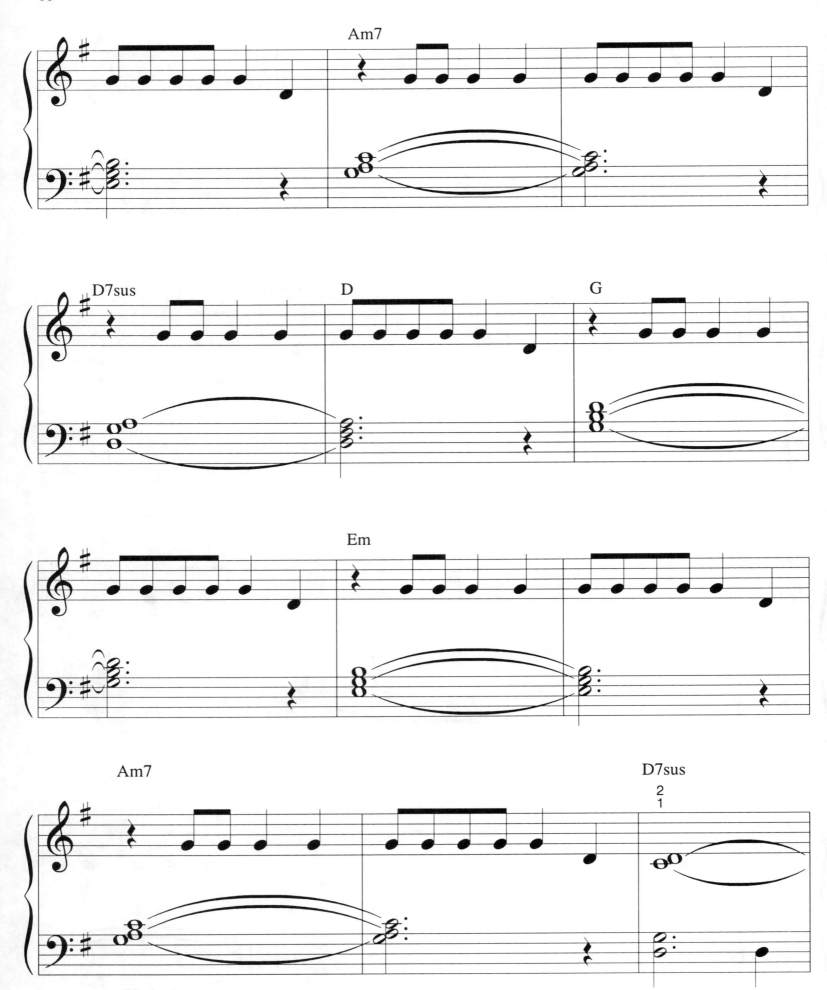

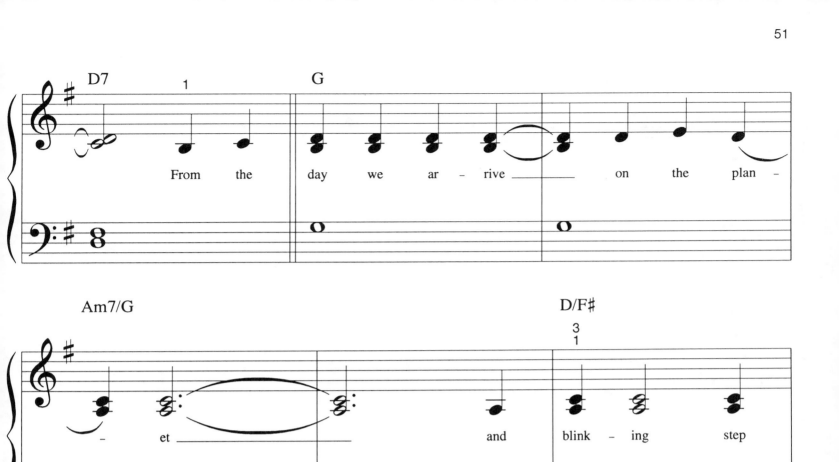

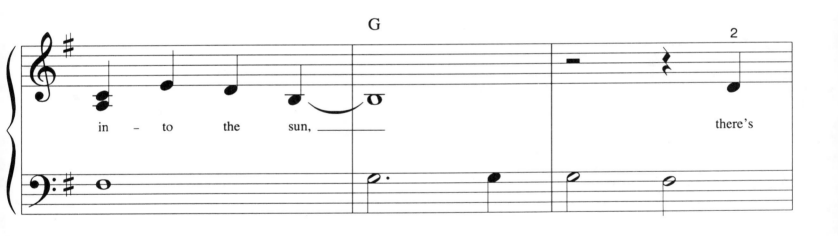

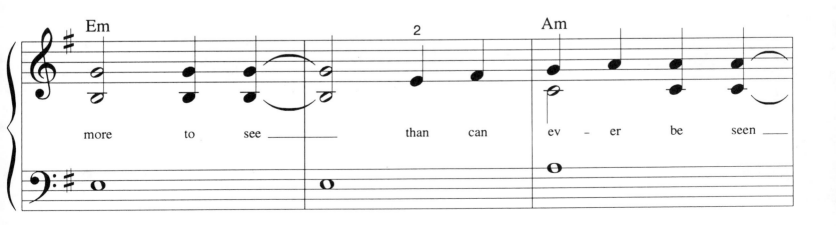

52

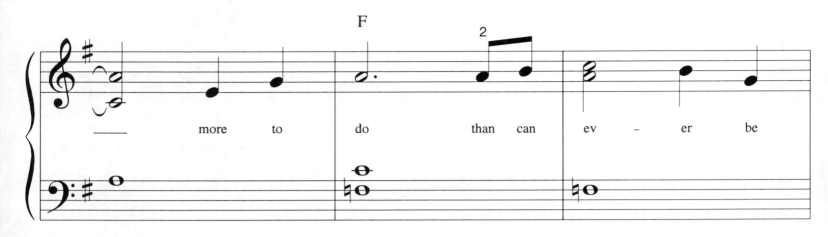

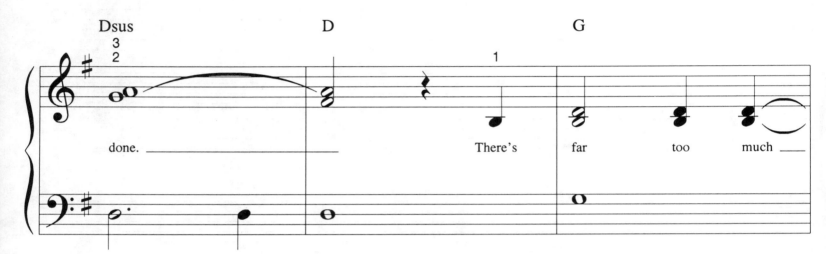

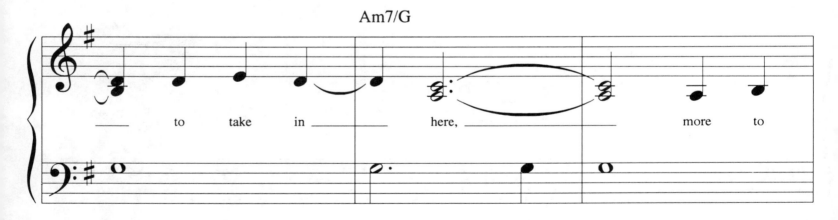

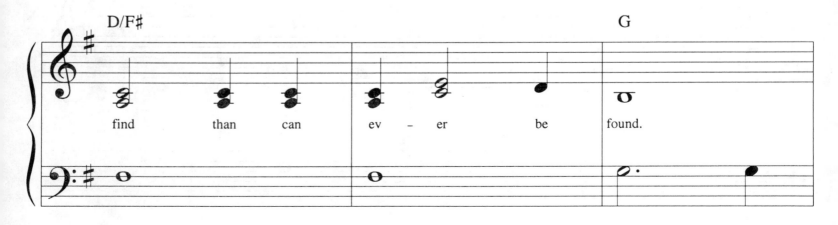

But the sun roll – ing high _____ through the
cresc.

sap – phi – re sky _____ keeps great and small on the

end – less round. _____ It's the cir – cle of

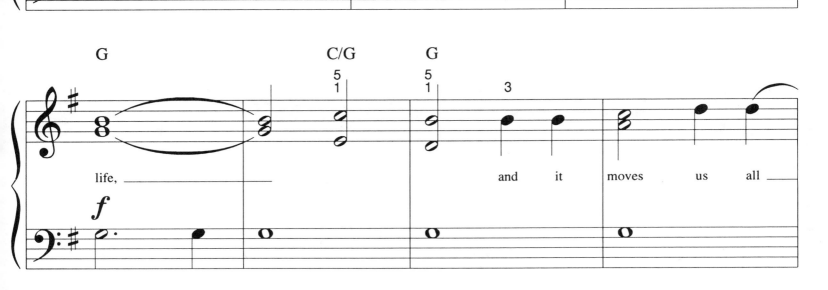

life, _____ and it moves us all _____

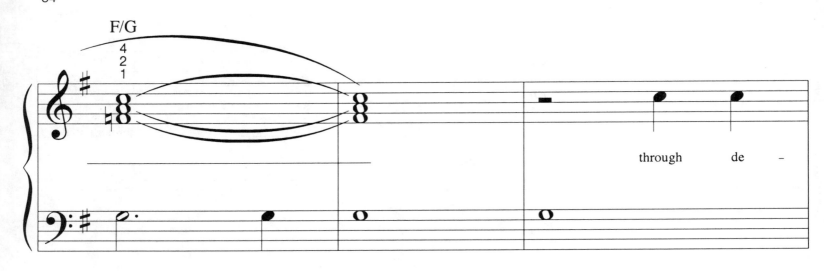

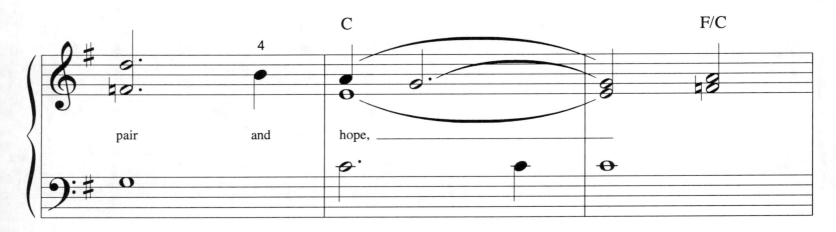

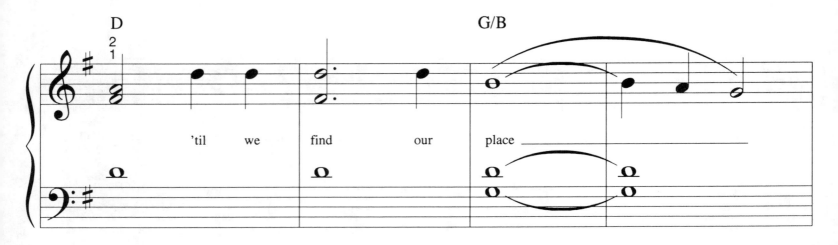

55

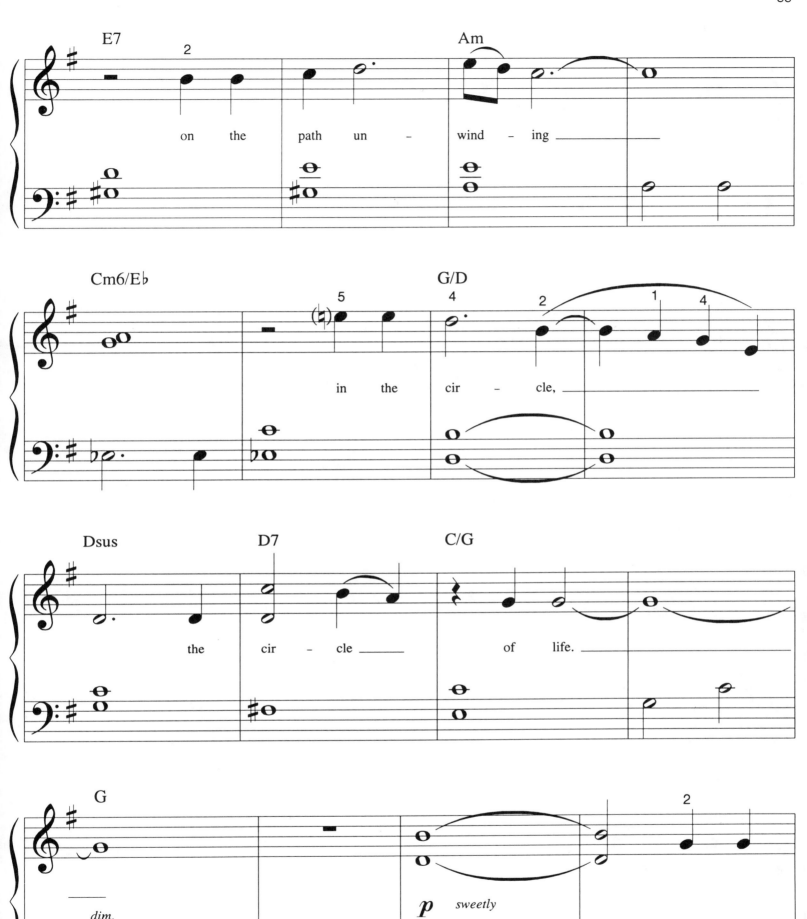

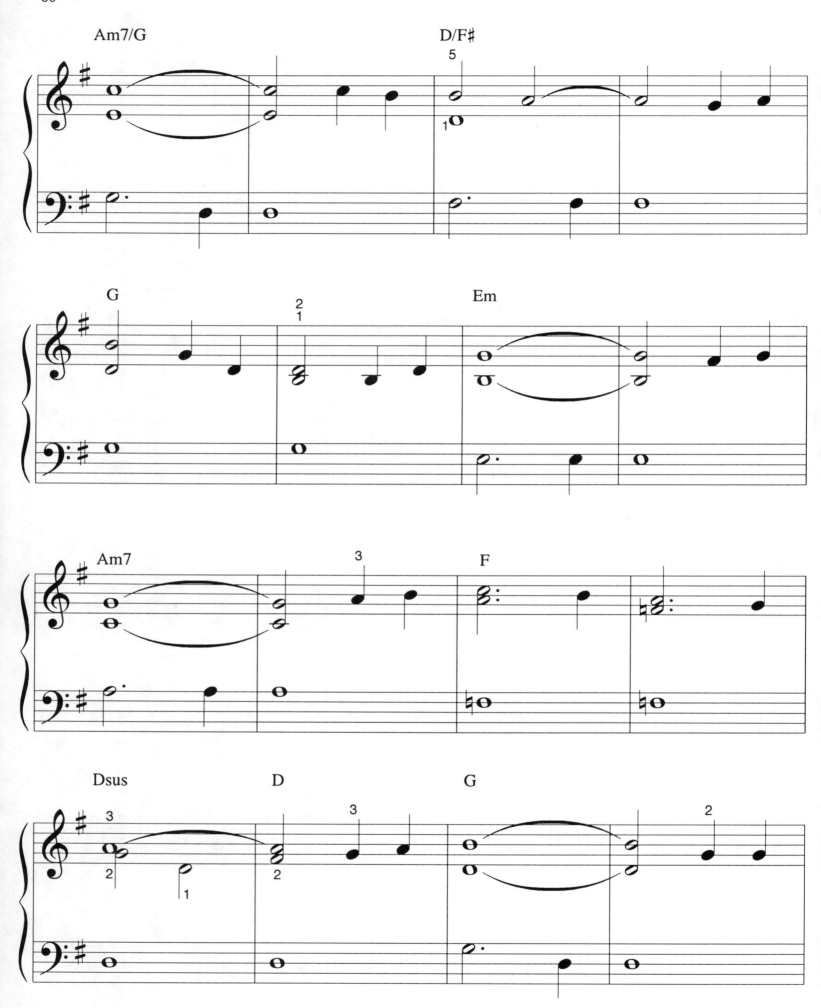

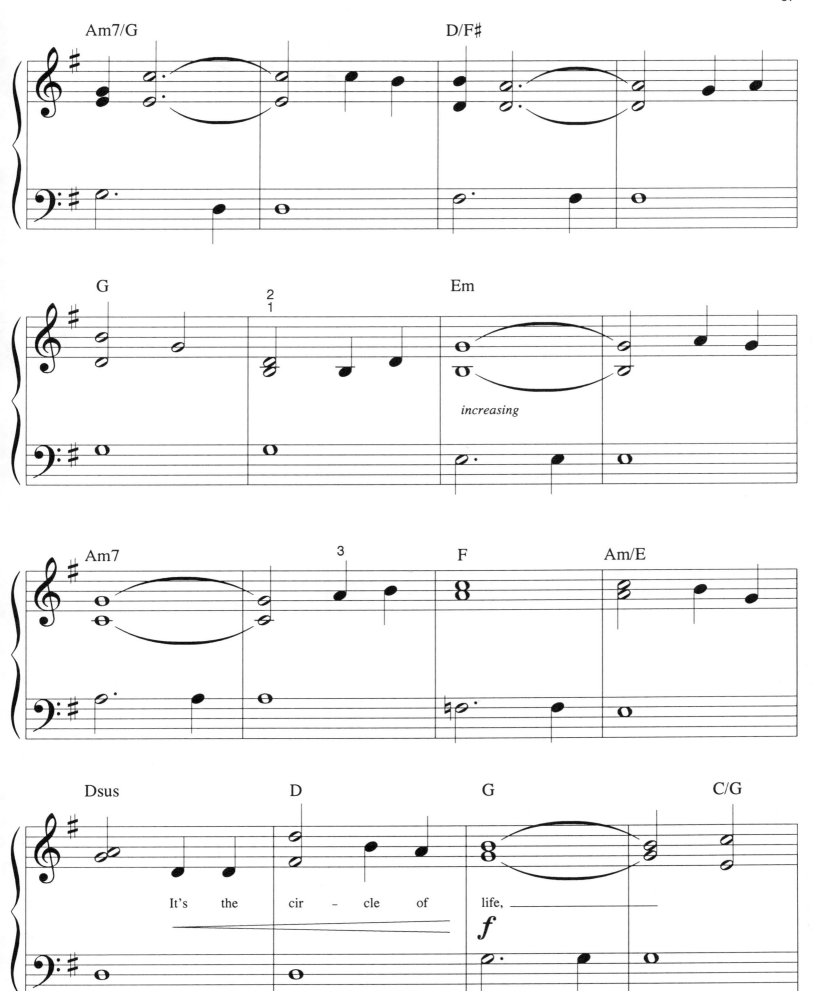

It's the cir - cle of life,

58

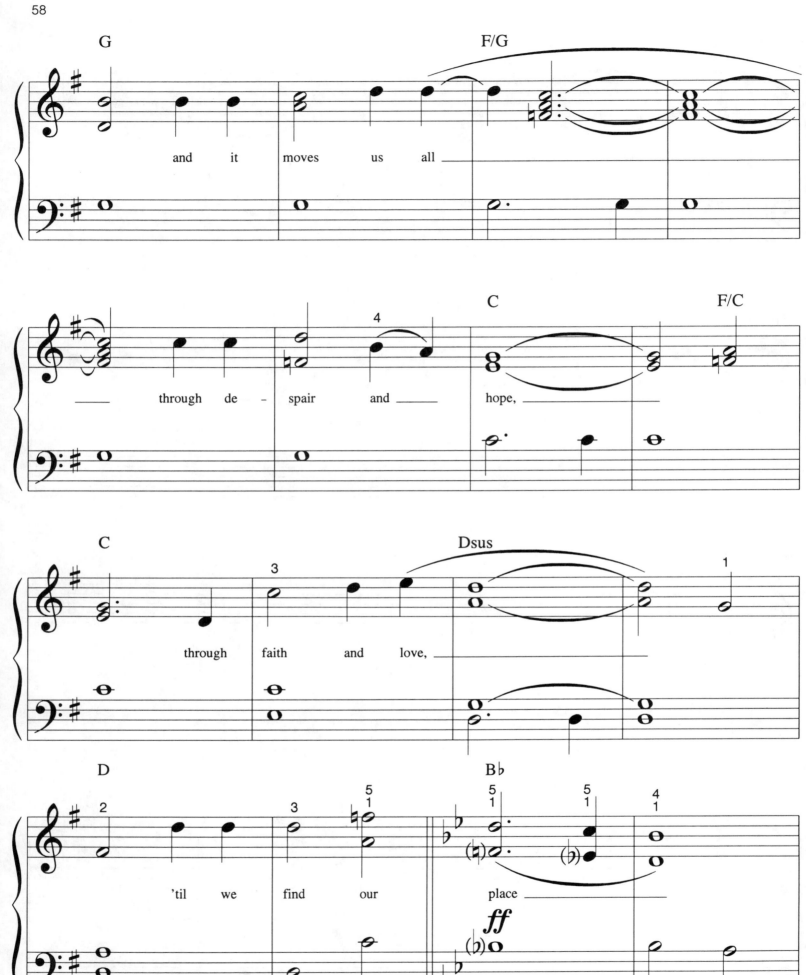

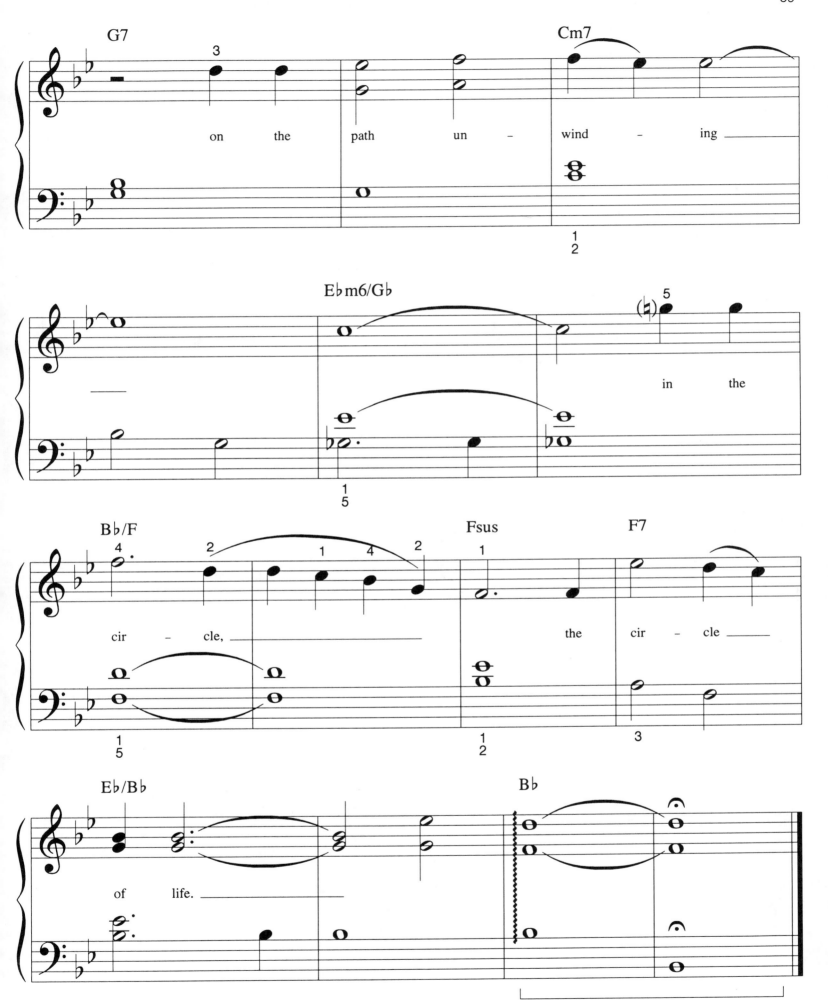

THE CRAWDAD SONG

Traditional

Brightly

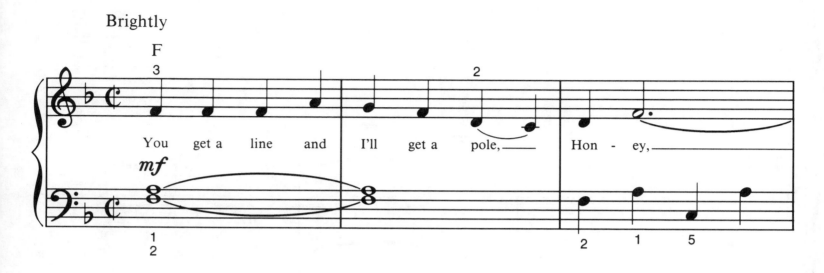

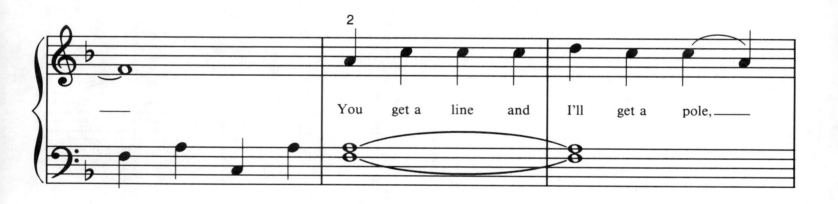

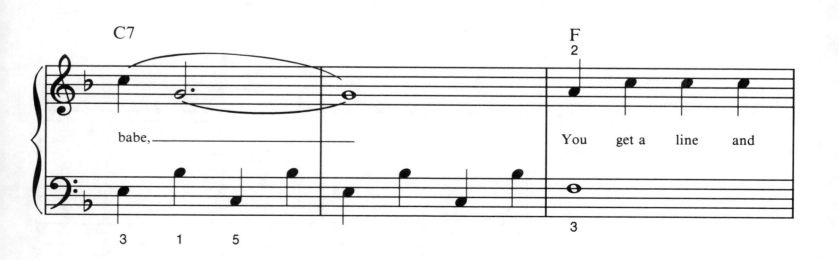

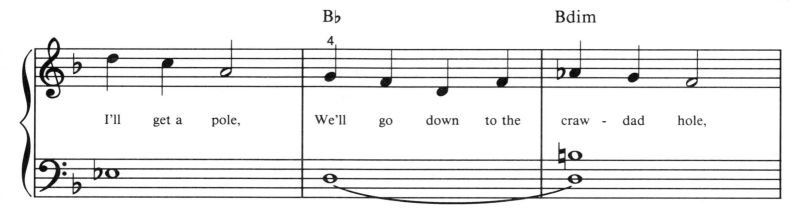

I'll get a pole, We'll go down to the craw - dad hole,

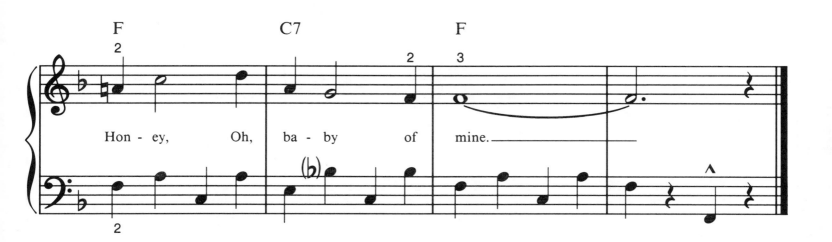

Hon - ey, Oh, ba - by of mine.

Additional Words

Yonder comes a man with a pack on his back, honey,
Yonder comes a man with a pack on his back, babe,
Yonder comes a man with a pack on his back,
Totin' all the crawdads he can pack,
Honey, Oh baby of mine.

(continue similarly)
Sittin' on the ice till my feet got hot (3x)
Watchin' those crawdads rack and trot

Crawdad, crawdad, better go to your hole (3x)
If I don't catch you, well bless my soul!

Whatcha gonna do when the lake runs dry? (3x)
Sit on the bank and watch the crawdads die.

Whatcha gonna do when your man (gal) runs away? (3x)
Get you a better one the very next day.

CRUELLA de VIL
from Walt Disney's 101 DALMATIONS

Words and Music by
MEL LEVEN

63

64

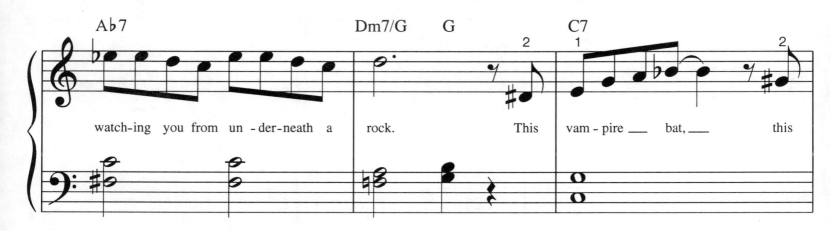

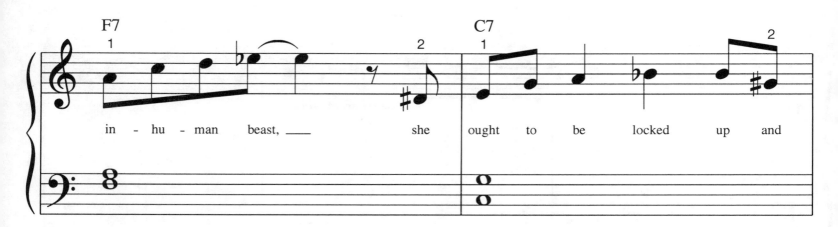

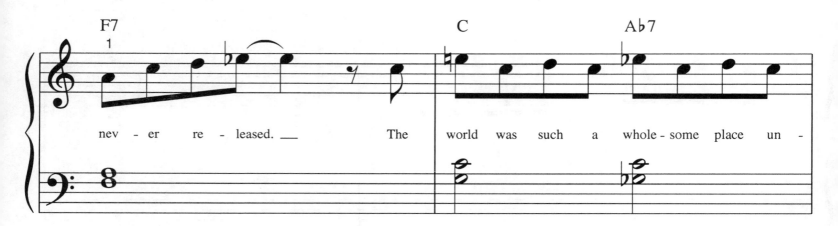

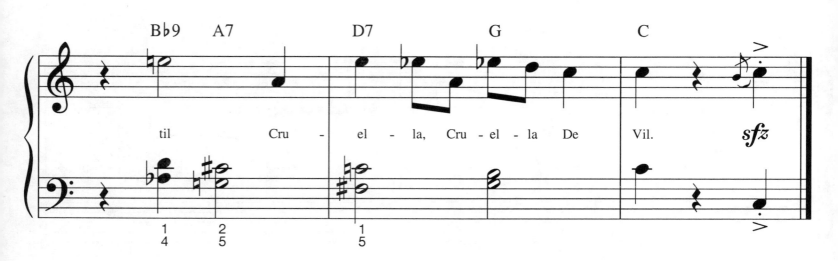

DOWN BY THE STATION

Traditional

DID YOU EVER SEE A LASSIE?

Anonymous

DITES-MOI
(TELL ME WHY)
from SOUTH PACIFIC

Lyrics by OSCAR HAMMERSTEIN II
Music by RICHARD RODGERS

EDELWEISS
from THE SOUND OF MUSIC

Lyrics by OSCAR HAMMERSTEIN II
Music by RICHARD RODGERS

Slow Waltz

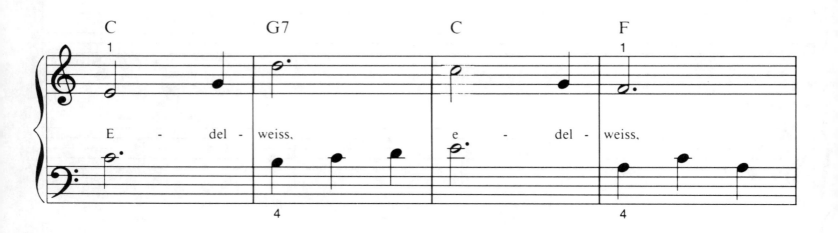

E - del - weiss,   e - del - weiss,

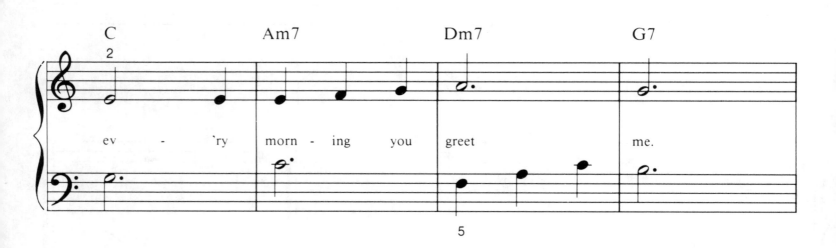

ev - 'ry morn - ing you greet me.

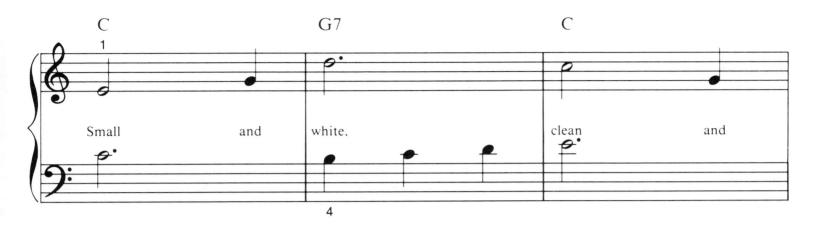

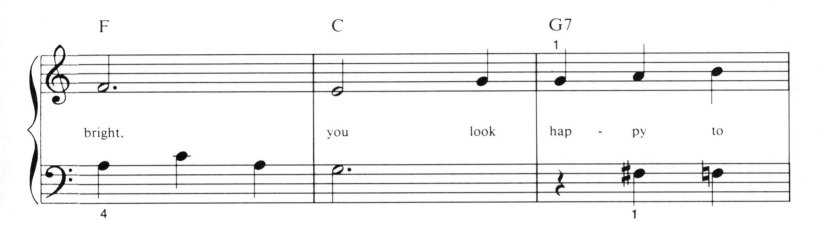

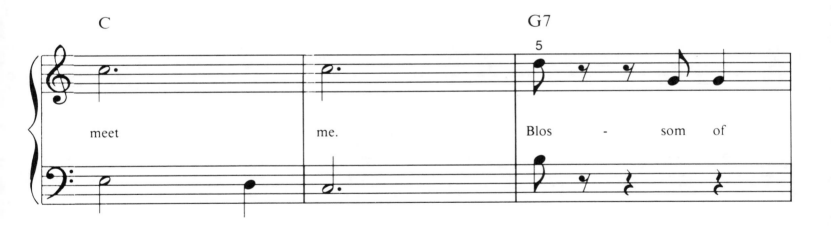

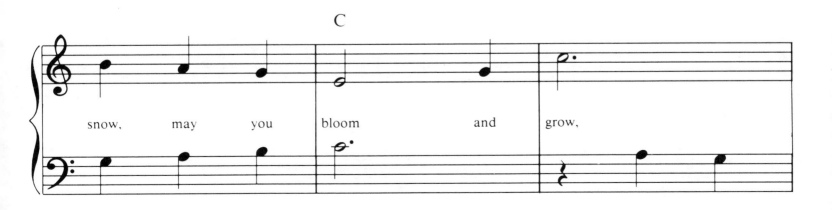

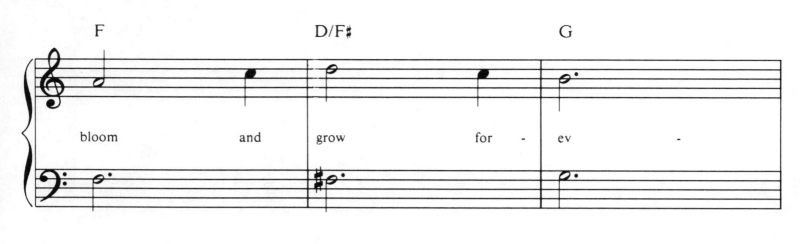

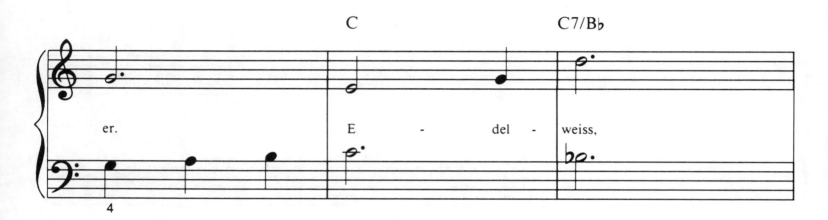

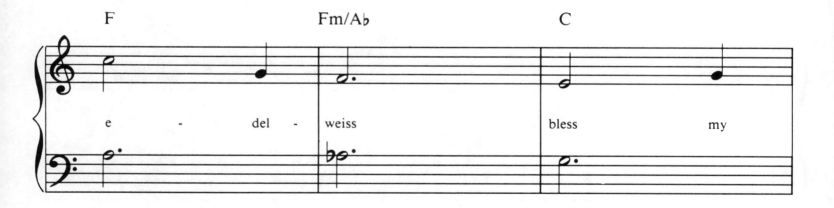

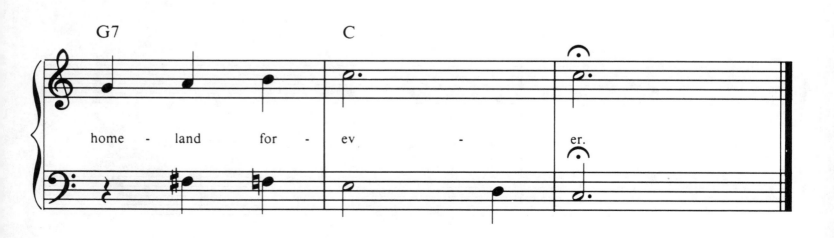

EVERYTHING IS BEAUTIFUL

Words and Music by
RAY STEVENS

74

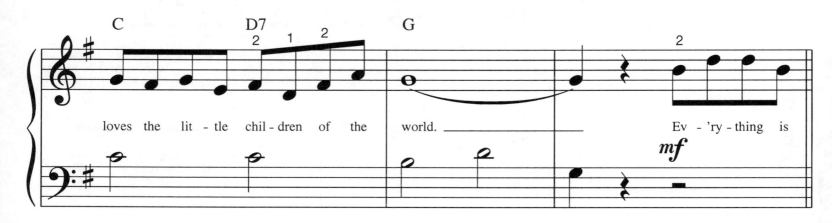

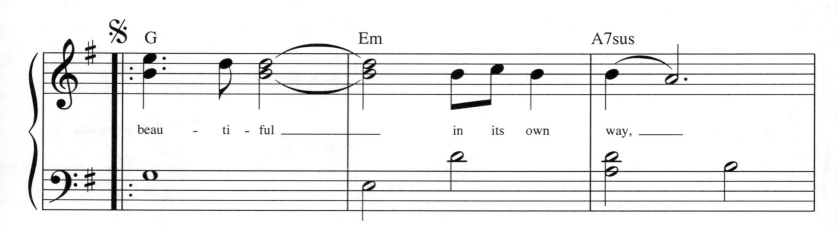

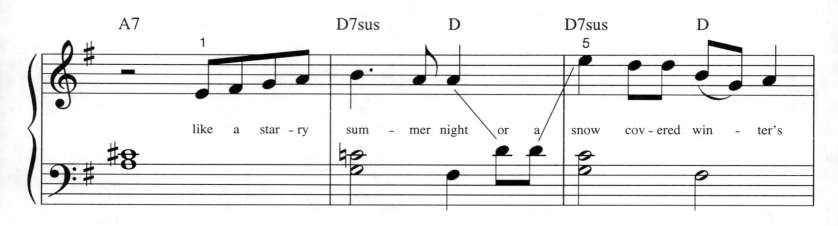

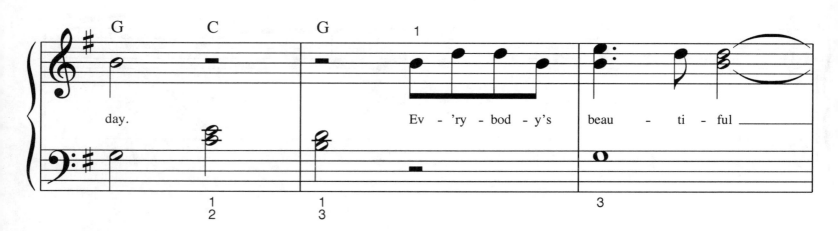

75

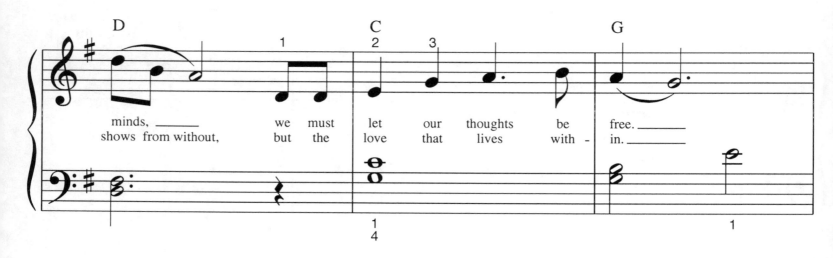

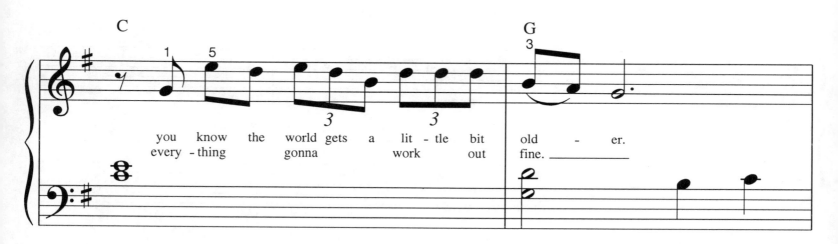

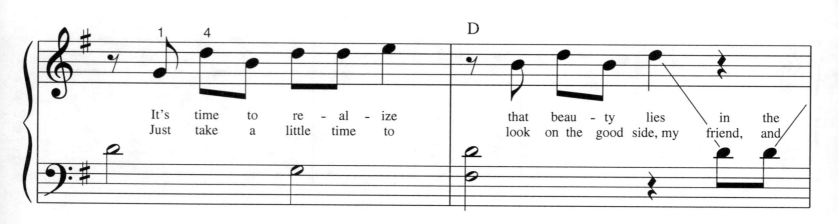

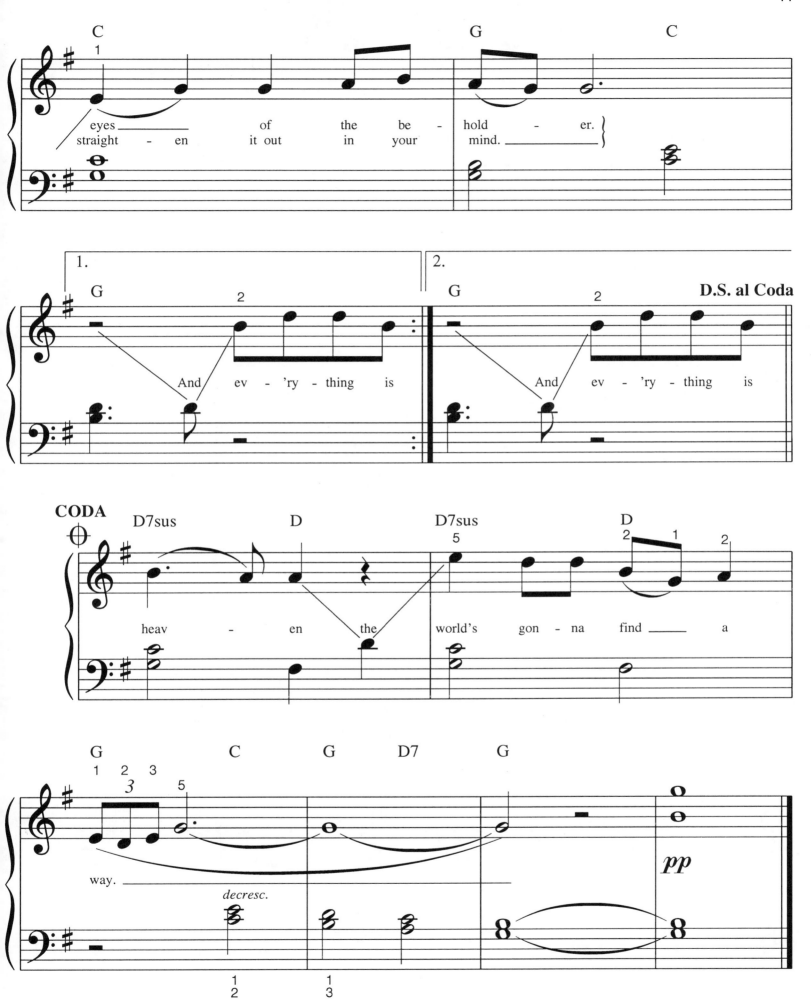

FEED THE BIRDS
from Walt Disney's MARY POPPINS

Words and Music by RICHARD M. SHERMAN
and ROBERT B. SHERMAN

Gentle Waltz

Feed the birds, tup - pence a bag,

Tup - pence, tup - pence, tup - pence a bag.

"Feed the birds," that's what she cries,

While o - ver - head her birds fill the skies. All a -

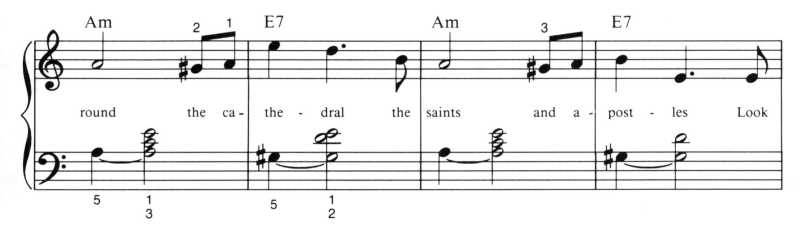

round the ca- the - dral the saints and a - post - les Look

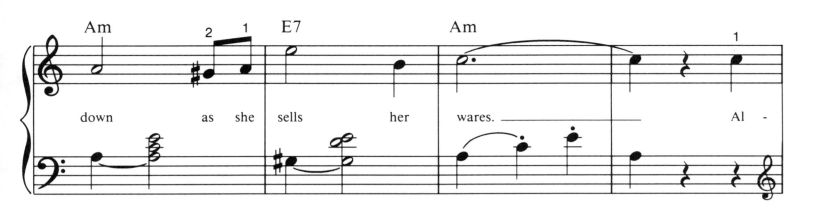

down as she sells her wares. _____ Al -

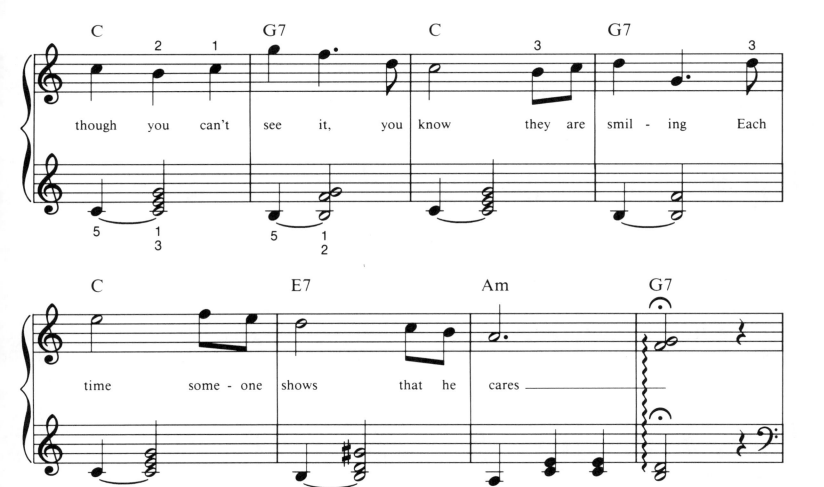

though you can't see it, you know they are smil - ing Each

time some - one shows that he cares _____

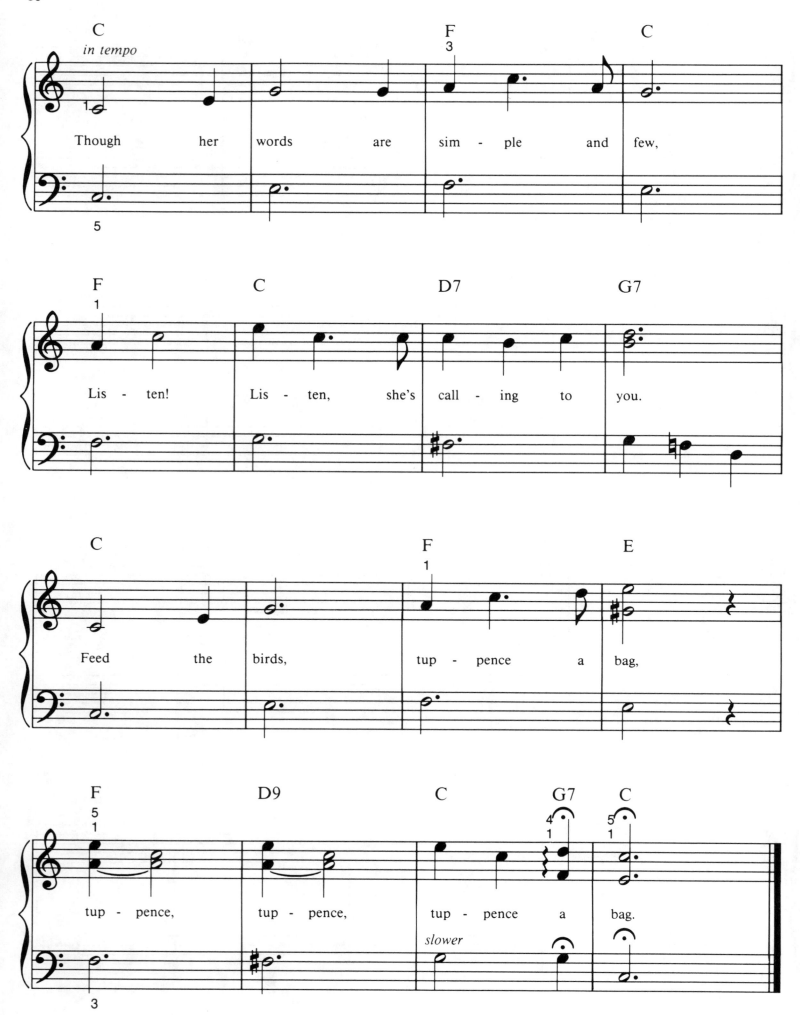

(Meet)
THE FLINTSTONES
from THE FLINTSTONES

Words and Music by W. HANNA,
J. BARBERA and H. CURTIN

Moderately

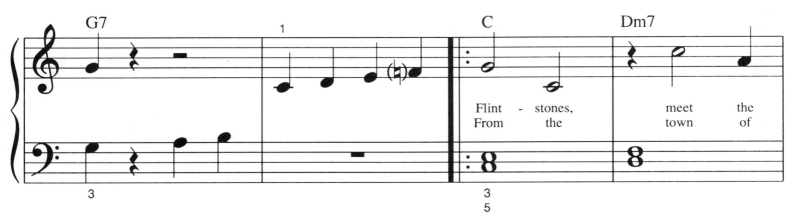

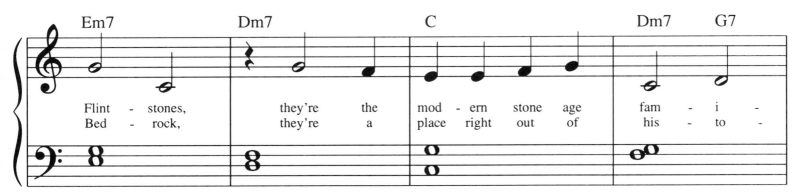

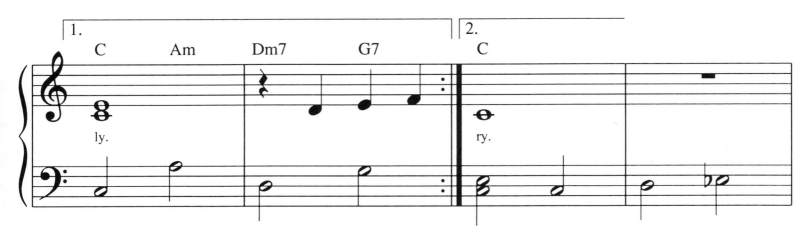

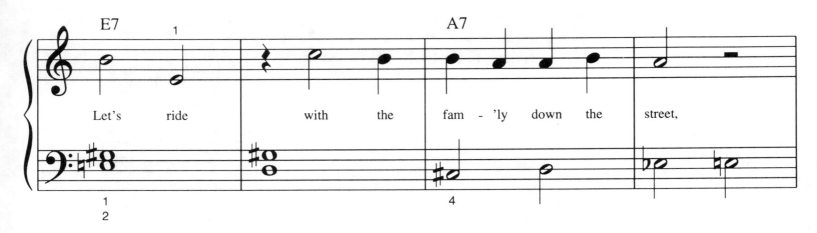

Let's ride with the fam - 'ly down the street,

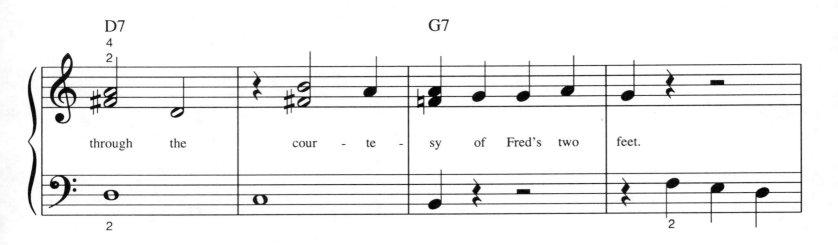

through the cour - te - sy of Fred's two feet.

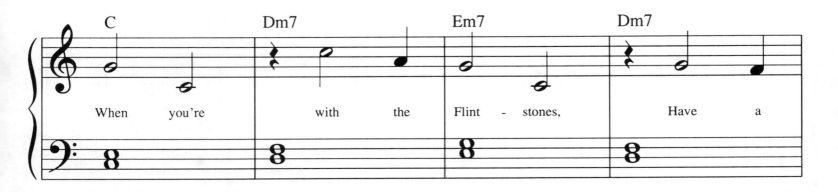

When you're with the Flint - stones, Have a

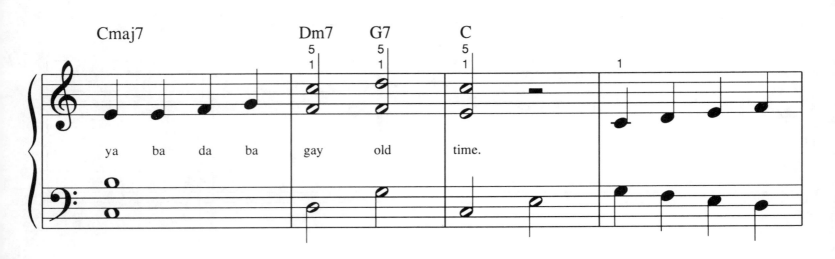

ya ba da ba gay old time.

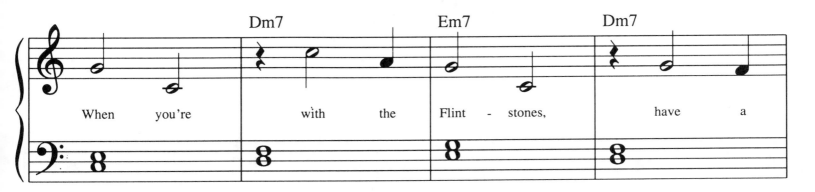

When you're with the Flint - stones, have a

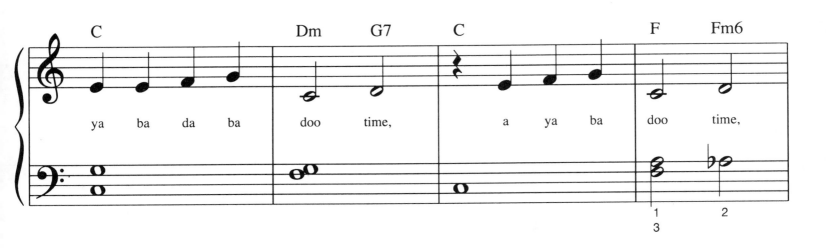

ya ba da ba doo time, a ya ba doo time,

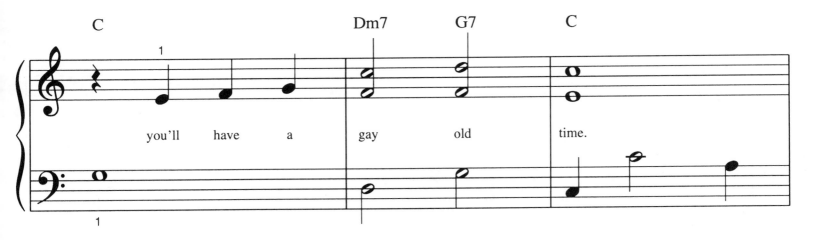

you'll have a gay old time.

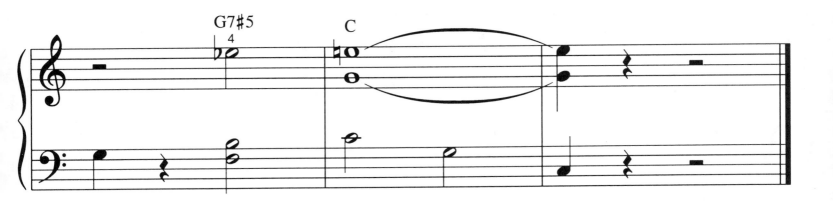

FROG WENT A-COURTIN'

Anonymous

F   1.-8.   9.

h'm,   H'm,   h'm.   2. He   h'm.
h'm,   H'm,   h'm.   3.-9.

3
5

Additional Lyrics

3. "Yes, Sir Frog, I sit and spin."
   H'm, h'm,
   H'm, h'm.
   "Yes, Sir Frog, I sit and spin.;"
   "Pray, Mister Froggie, won't you walk in?"
   H'm, h'm,
   H'm, h'm.

4. The frog said, "My dear, I've come to see."
   H'm, h'm,
   H'm, h'm.
   The frog said, "My dear, I've come to see
   If you, Miss Mousie, will marry me."
   H'm, h'm,
   H'm, h'm.

5. "I don't know what to say to that."
   H'm, h'm,
   H'm, h'm.
   "I don't know what to say to that.
   Till I speak with my Uncle Rat."
   H'm, h'm,
   H'm, h'm.

6. When Uncle Rat came riding home.
   H'm, h'm,
   H'm, h'm.
   When Uncle Rat came riding home.
   Said he, "Who's been here since I've been gone?"
   H'm, h'm,
   H'm, h'm.

7. "A fine young froggie has been here."
   H'm, h'm,
   H'm, h'm.
   "A fine young froggie has been here.
   He means to marry me it's clear."
   H'm, h'm,
   H'm, h'm.

8. So Uncle Rat, he rode to town.
   H'm, h'm,
   H'm, h'm.
   So Uncle Rat, he rode to town
   And bought his niece a wedding gown.
   H'm, h'm,
   H'm, h'm.

9. The frog and mouse they went to France.
   H'm, h'm,
   H'm, h'm.
   The frog and mouse they went to France.
   And that's the end of my romance.
   H'm, h'm,
   H'm, h'm.

GO IN AND OUT THE WINDOW

Traditional

87

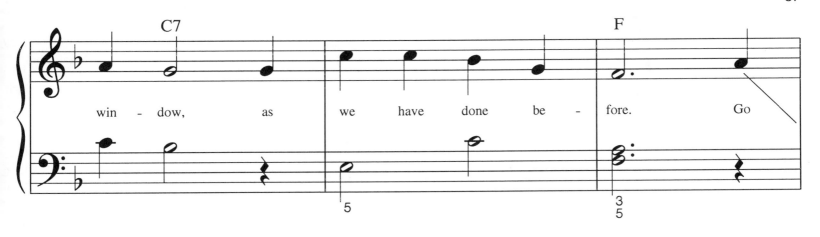

win - dow, as we have done be - fore. Go

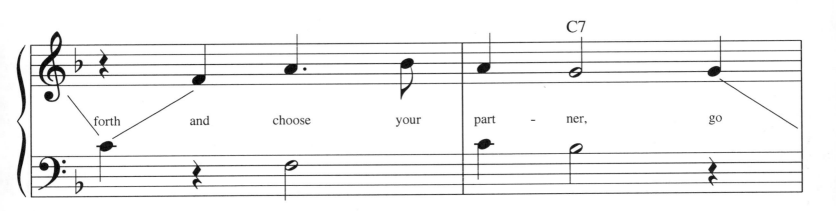

forth and choose your part - ner, go

forth and choose your part - ner. Go forth and choose your

part - ner, as we have done be - fore.

GO TELL AUNT RHODY

Traditional

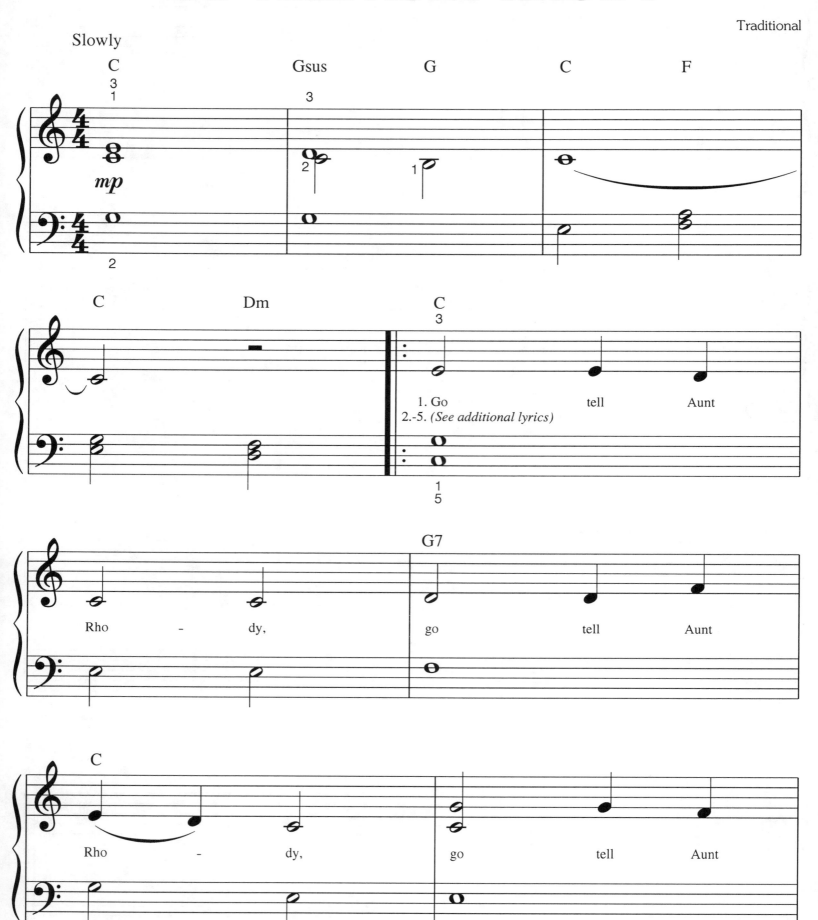

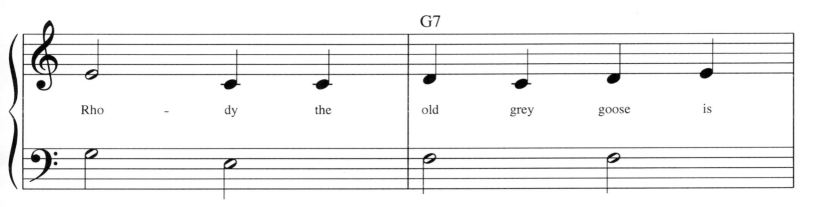

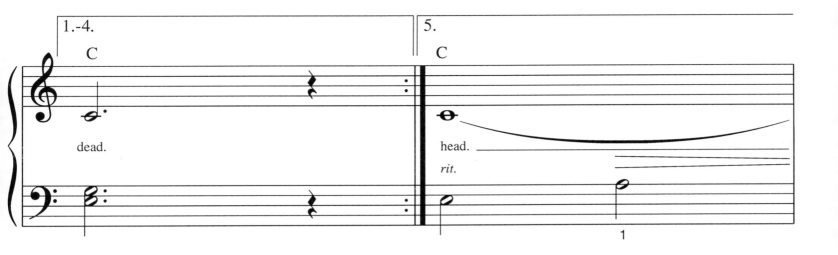

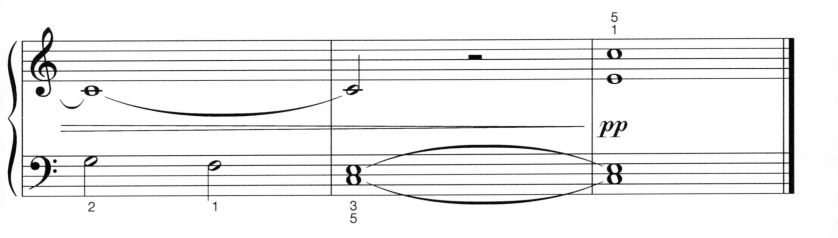

Additional Lyrics

2. The one she was saving, *(three times)*
   To make a feather bed.

3. The gander is weeping, *(three times)*
   Because his wife is dead.

4. The goslings are crying, *(three times)*
   Because their mama's dead.

5. She died in the water, *(three times)*
   With her heels above her head.

GETTING TO KNOW YOU
from THE KING AND I

Lyrics by OSCAR HAMMERSTEIN II
Music by RICHARD RODGERS

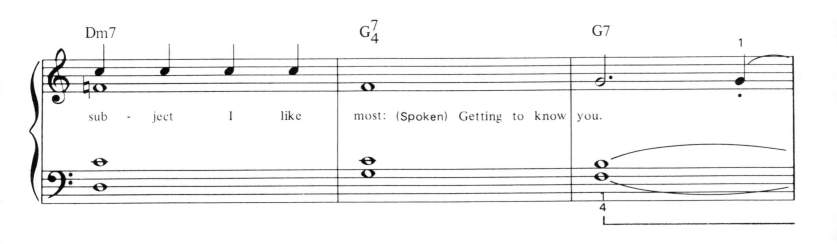

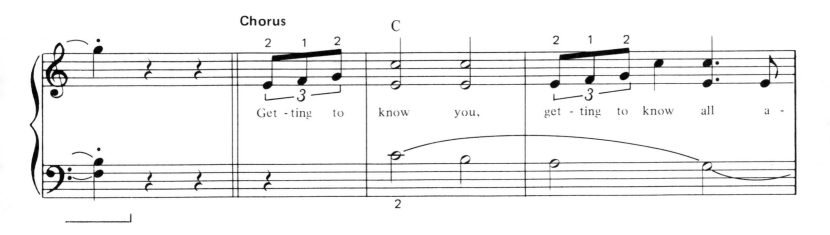

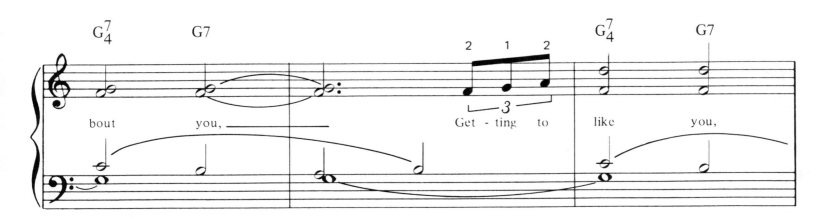

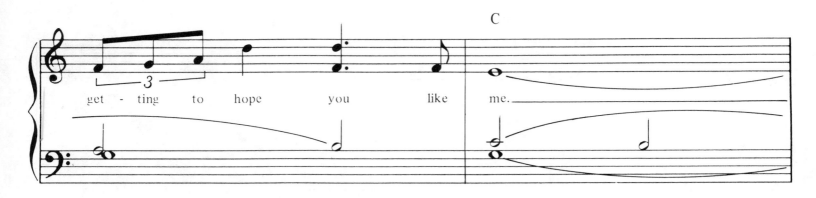

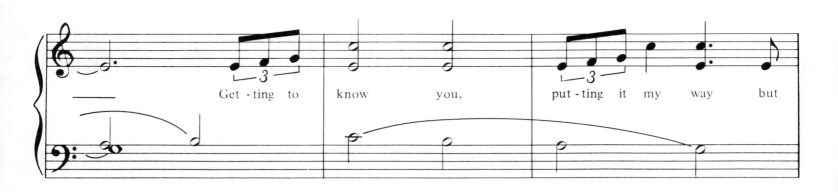

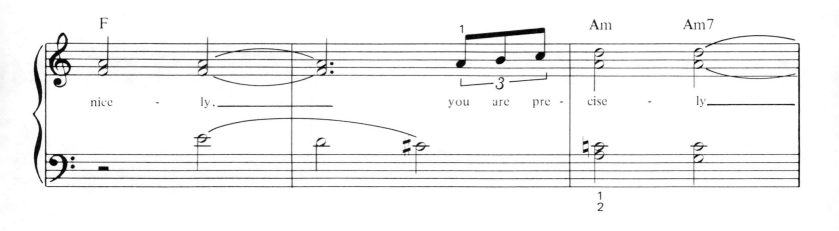

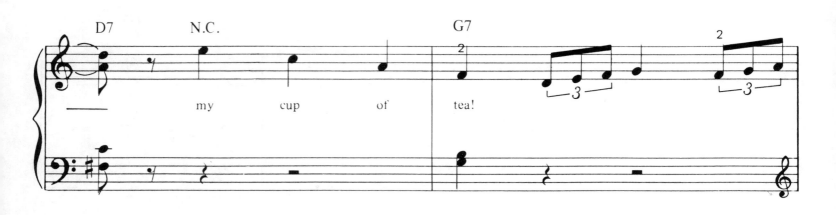

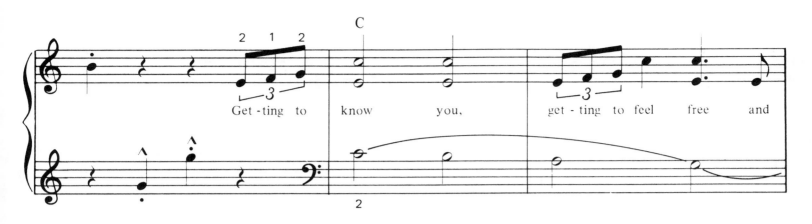

Get-ting to know you, get-ting to feel free and

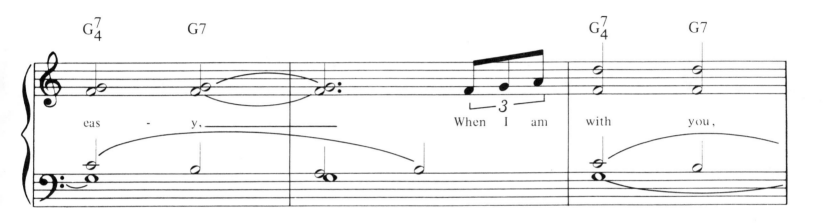

eas - y,____ When I am with you,

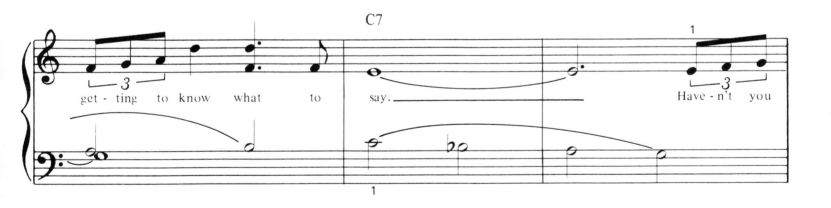

get-ting to know what to say._____ Have-n't you

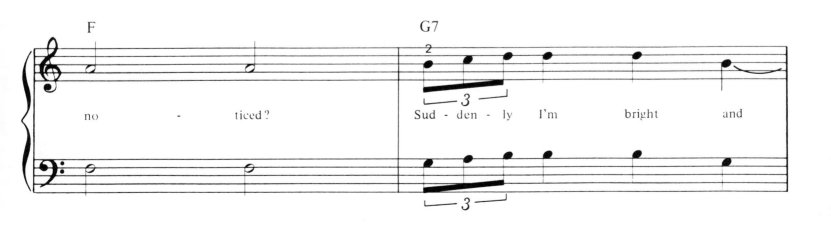

no - ticed? Sud - den - ly I'm bright and

94

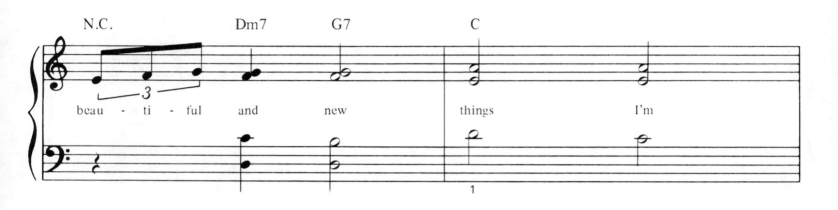

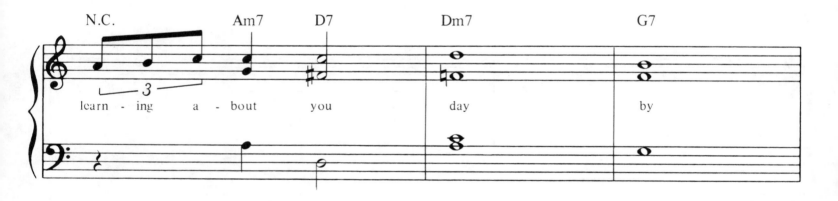

HEIGH-HO
the Dwarfs' Marching Song from SNOW WHITE AND THE SEVEN DWARFS

Words by LARRY MOREY
Music by FRANK CHURCHILL

97

HAPPY TRAILS
from the Television Series THE ROY ROGERS SHOW

Words and Music by
DALE EVANS

HEART AND SOUL
from the Paramount Short Subject A SONG IS BORN

Words by FRANK LOESSER
Music by HOAGY CARMICHAEL

tight and stole a kiss in the night. Heart and soul, _____

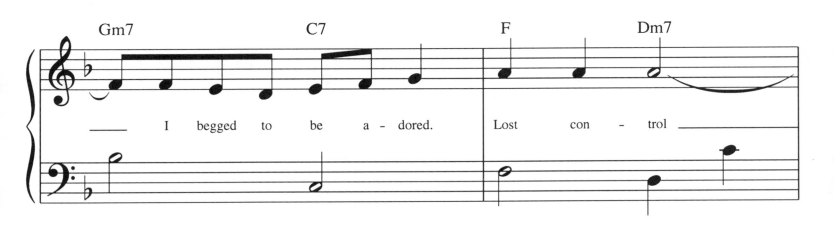

_____ I begged to be a - dored. Lost con - trol _____

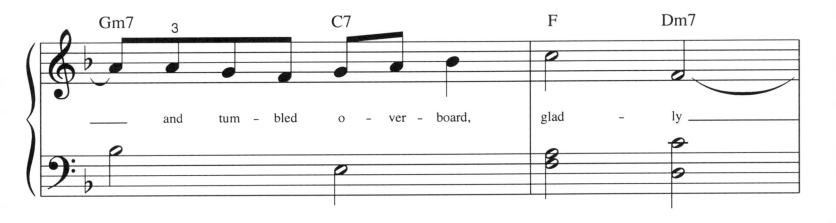

_____ and tum - bled o - ver - board, glad - ly _____

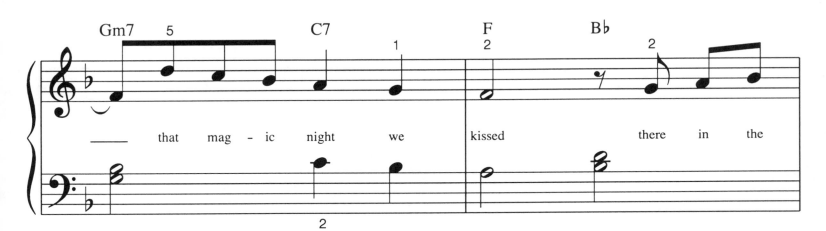

_____ that mag - ic night we kissed there in the

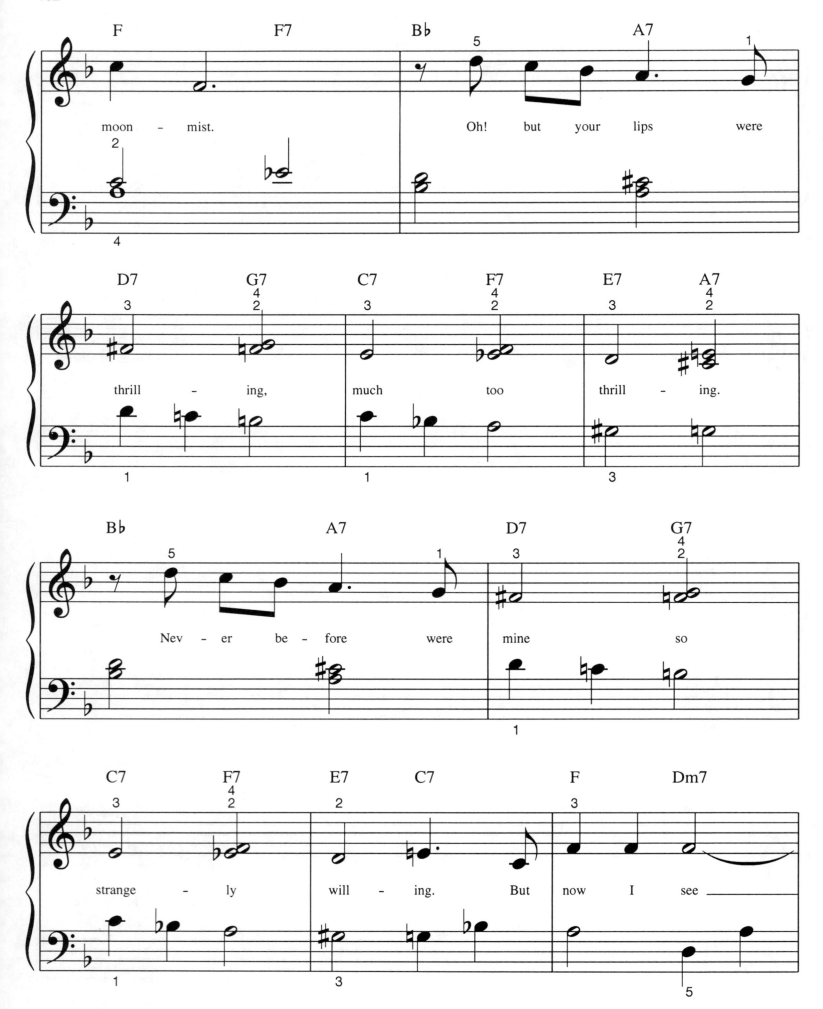

HI-DIDDLE-DEE-DEE
(AN ACTOR'S LIFE FOR ME)
from Walt Disney's PINOCCHIO

Words by NED WASHINGTON
Music by LEIGH HARLINE

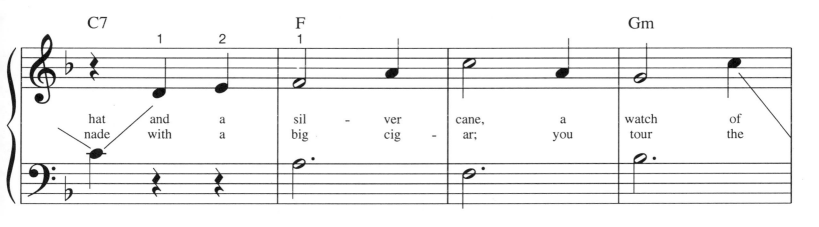

hat and a sil - ver cane, a watch of
nade with a big cig - ar; you tour of the

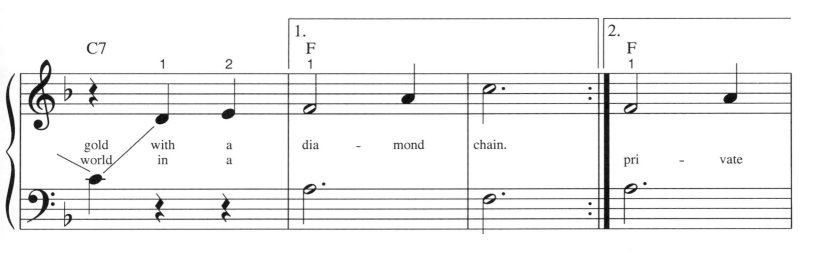

gold with a dia - mond chain.
world in a

pri - vate

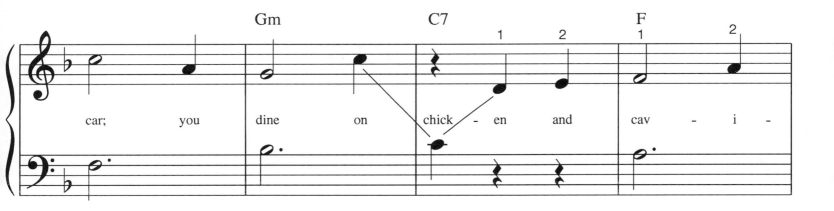

car; you dine on chick - en and cav - i -

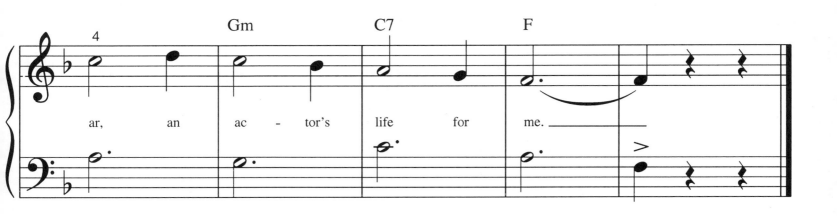

ar, an ac - tor's life for me. ___

HOME ON THE RANGE

Traditional

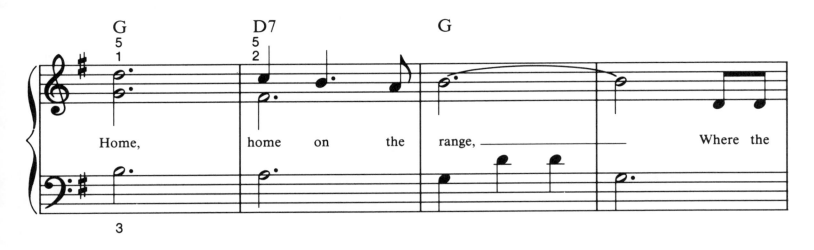

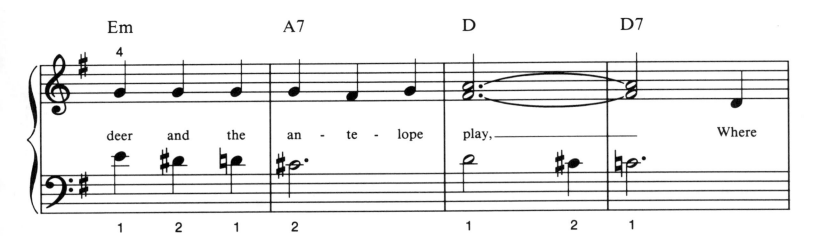

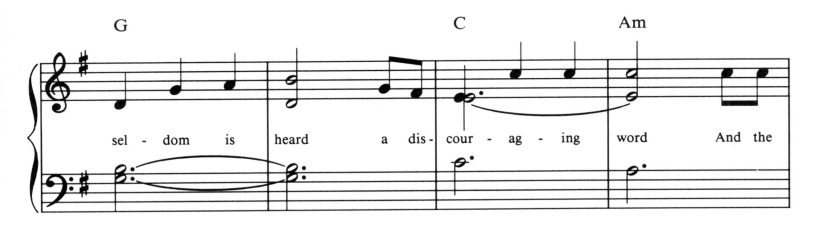

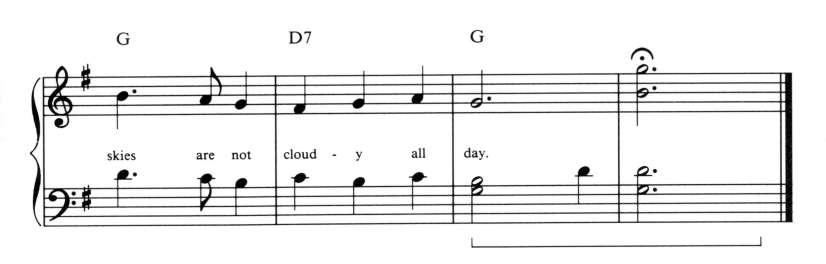

HOUSE AT POOH CORNER

Words and Music by
KENNY LOGGINS

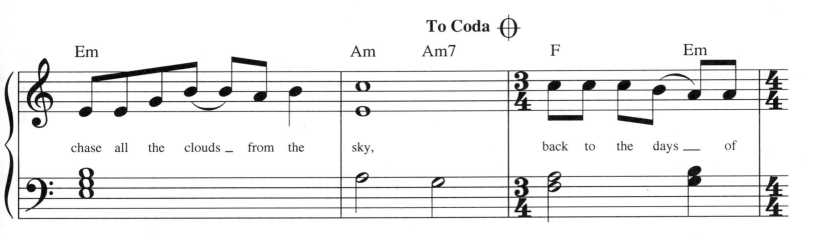

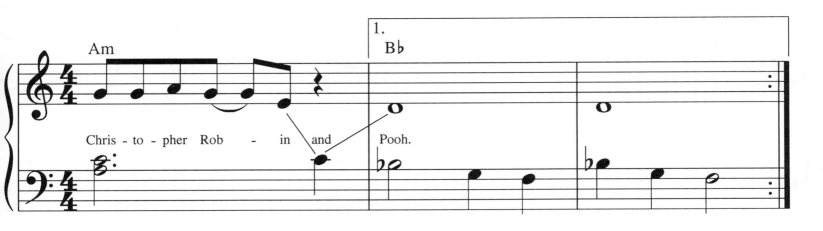

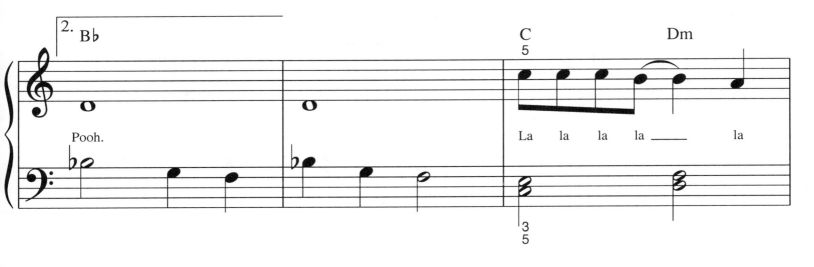

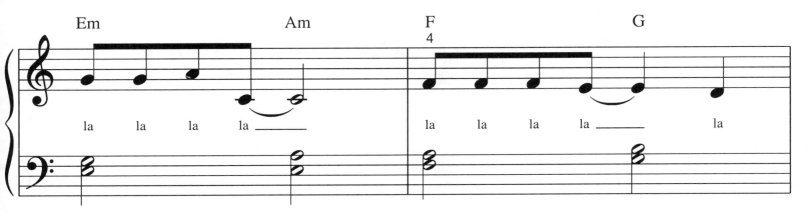

112

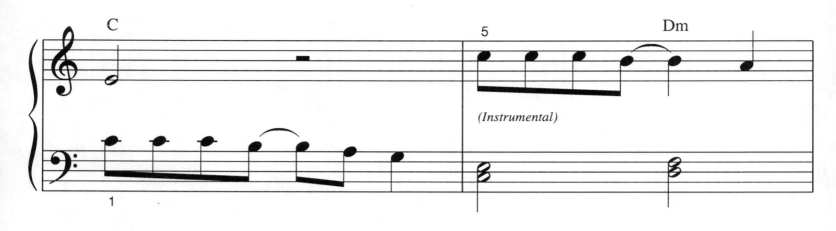

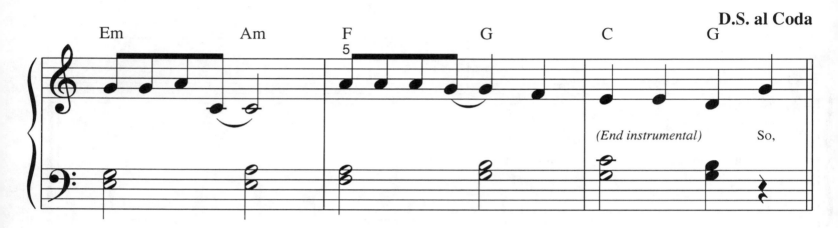

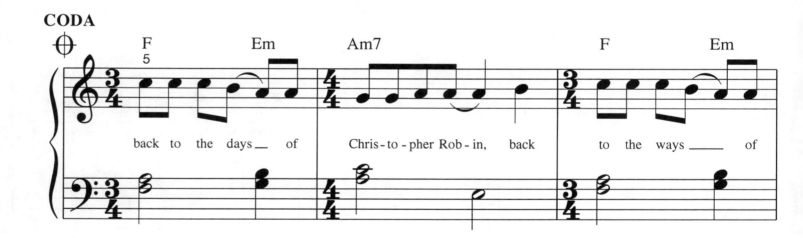

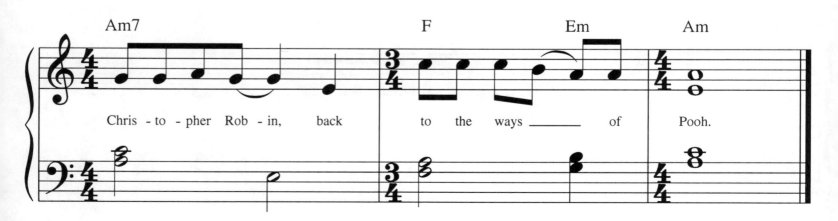

I DON'T WANT TO LIVE ON THE MOON

from the Television Series SESAME STREET

Words and Music by
JEFF MOSS

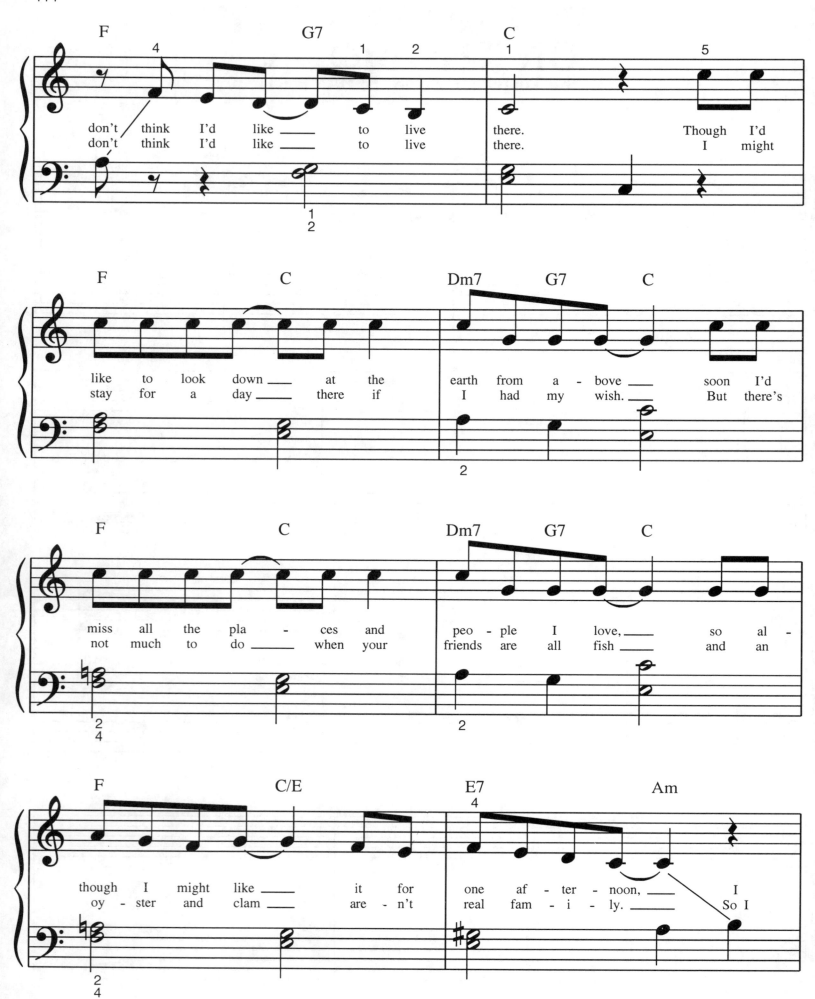

I LOVE TRASH

from the Television Series SESAME STREET

Words and Music by
JEFF MOSS

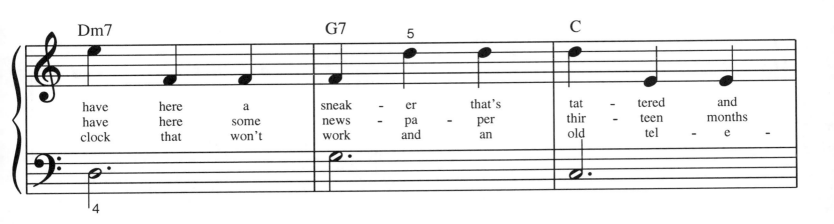

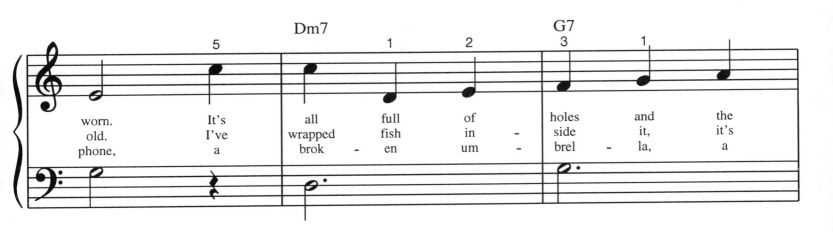

IT'S RAINING, IT'S POURING

Traditional

I'M POPEYE THE SAILOR MAN
Theme from the Paramount Cartoon POPEYE THE SAILOR

Words and Music by
SAMMY LERNER

Sail - or Man. _____ I'm one tough Ga - zoo - kus Which
Sail - or Man. _____ He's one tough Ga - zoo - kus Which

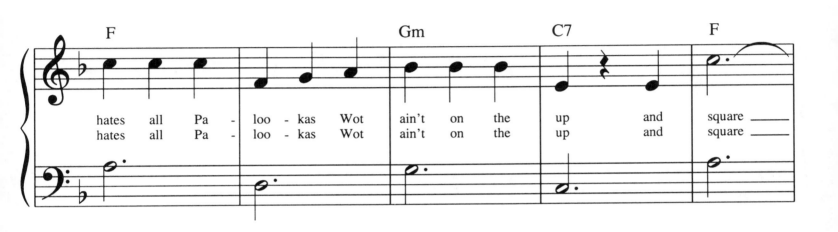

hates all Pa - loo - kas Wot ain't on the up and square _____
hates all Pa - loo - kas Wot ain't on the up up and square _____

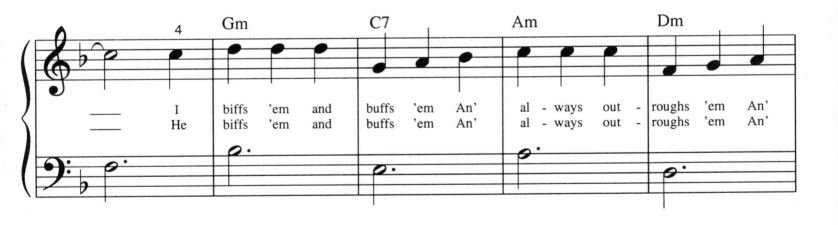

_____ I biffs 'em and buffs 'em An' al - ways out - roughs 'em An'
_____ He biffs 'em and buffs 'em An' al - ways out - roughs 'em An'

none of 'em gits no - where. _____ If an - y one
none of 'em gits no - where. _____ If an - y one

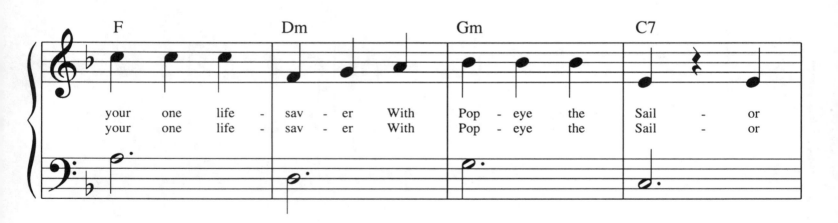

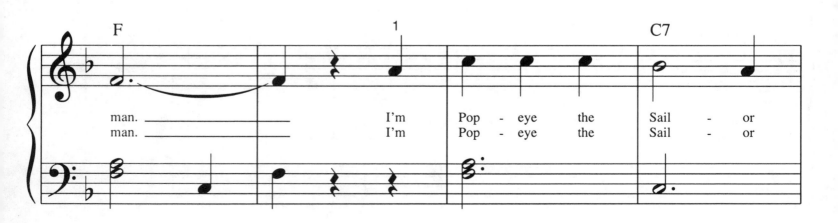

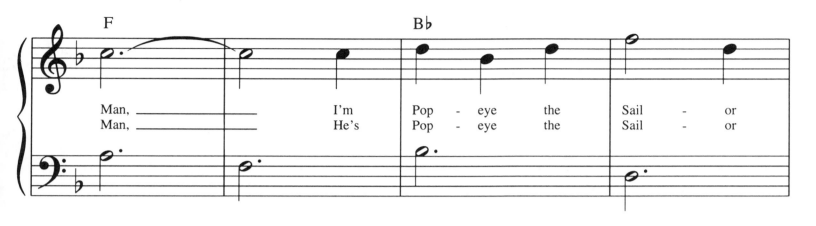

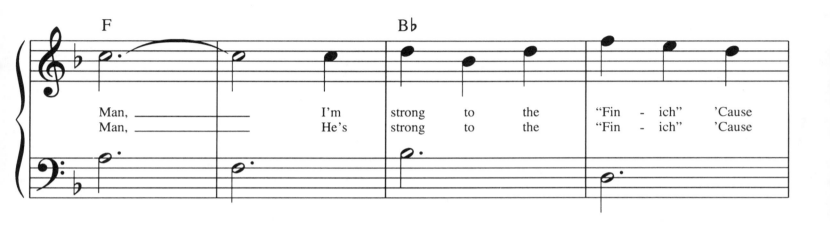

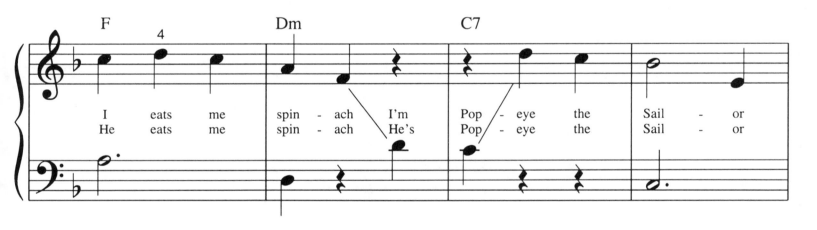

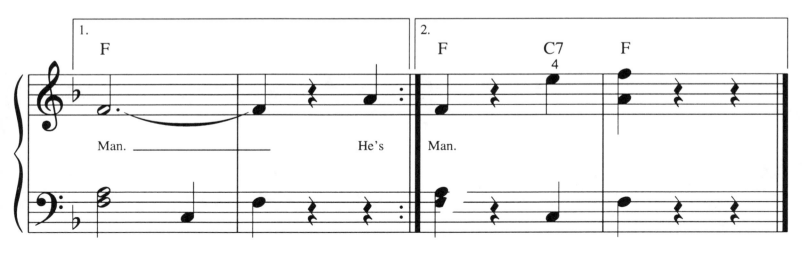

I'VE GOT NO STRINGS
from Walt Disney's PINOCCHIO

Words by NED WASHINGTON
Music by LEIGH HARLINE

JESUS LOVES ME

Traditional

Rather fast

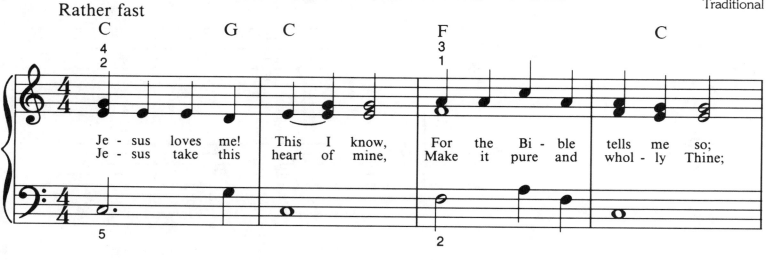

Je - sus loves me! This I know, For the Bi - ble tells me so;
Je - sus take this heart of mine, Make it pure and whol - ly Thine;

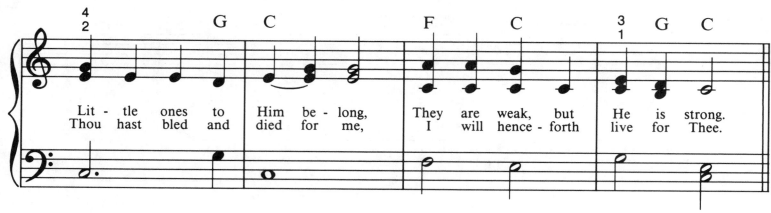

Lit - tle ones to Him be - long, They are weak, but He is strong.
Thou hast bled and died for me, I will hence - forth live for Thee.

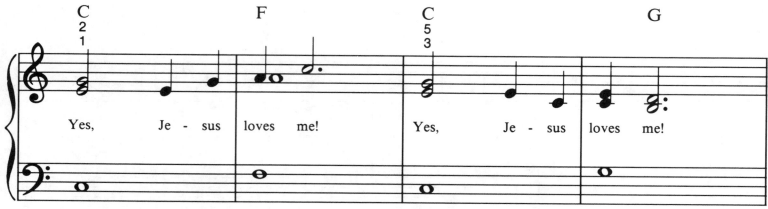

Yes, Je - sus loves me! Yes, Je - sus loves me!

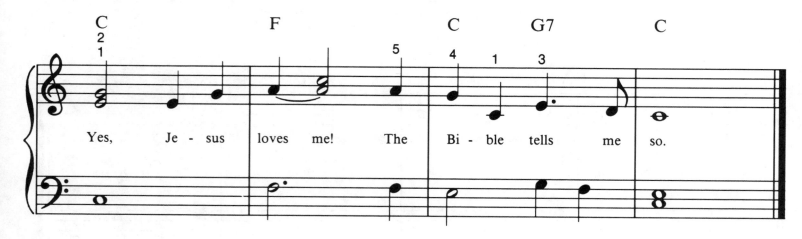

Yes, Je - sus loves me! The Bi - ble tells me so.

LI'L LIZA JANE

Words and Music by
COUNTESS ADA de LACHAU

Additional Words

Liza Jane done come to me...
We're as happy as can be...

Come, my love, and live with me...
I will take good care of thee...

House and lot in Baltimore...
Lots of children 'round the door...

LAZY MARY, WILL YOU GET UP?

Traditional

La - zy
Oh, no,

Ma - ry, will you get up, will
Moth - er, I won't get up, I

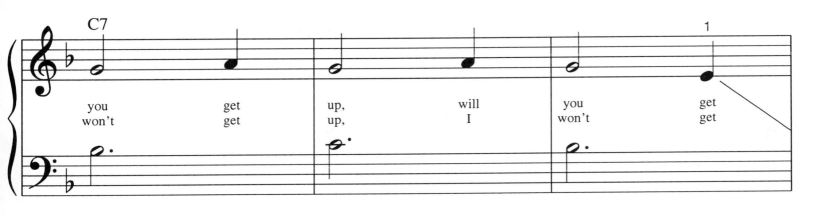

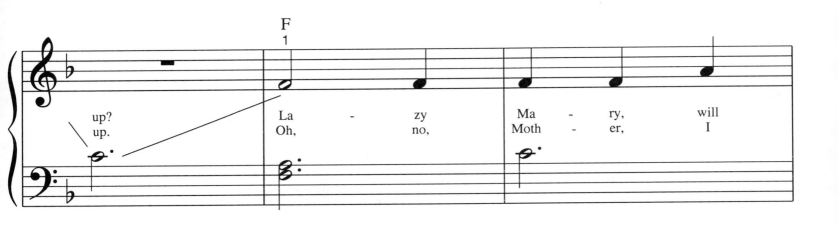

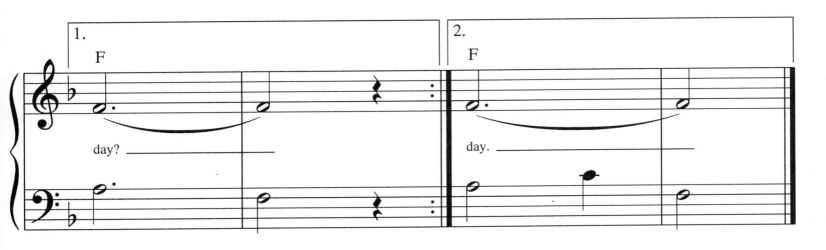

LET'S GO FLY A KITE
from Walt Disney's MARY POPPINS

Words and Music by RICHARD M. SHERMAN
and ROBERT B. SHERMAN

MAGIC PENNY

Words and Music by
MALVINA REYNOLDS

It's just like a mag - ic pen - ny, hold it tight and you

won't have an - y. Lend it, spend it, and you'll have so man - y, they'll

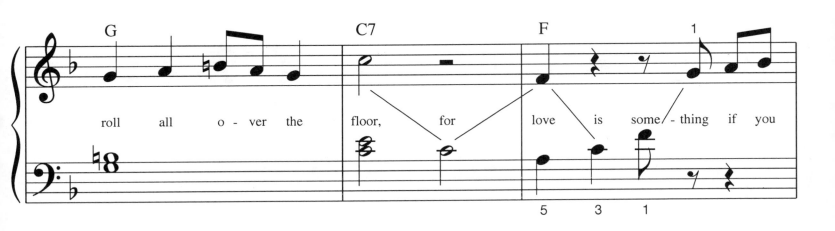

roll all o - ver the floor, for love is some - thing if you

give it a - way, ___ give it a - way, ___ give it a - way, ___

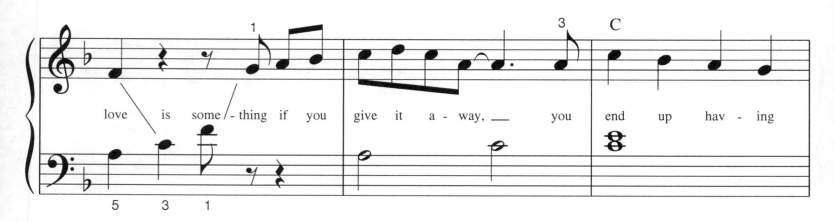

love is some - thing if you give it a - way, ___ you end up hav - ing

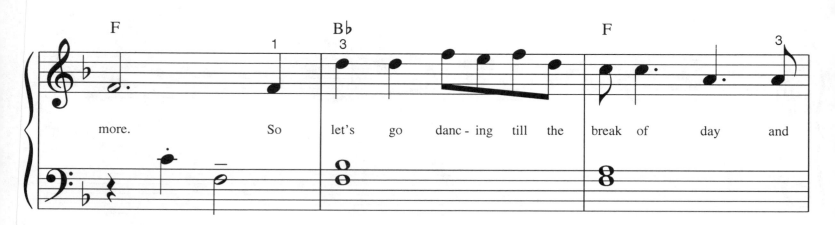

more. So let's go danc - ing till the break of day and

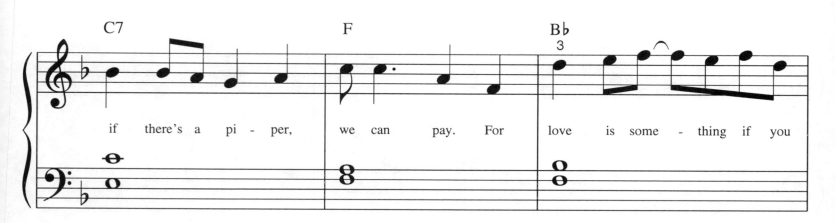

if there's a pi - per, we can pay. For love is some - thing if you

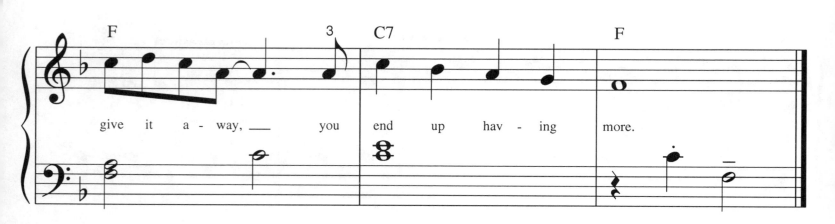

give it a - way, ___ you end up hav - ing more.

THE MARVELOUS TOY

Words and Music by
TOM PAXTON

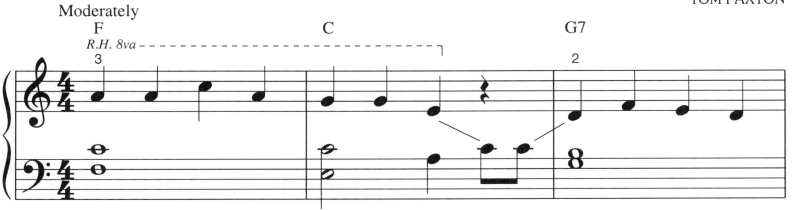

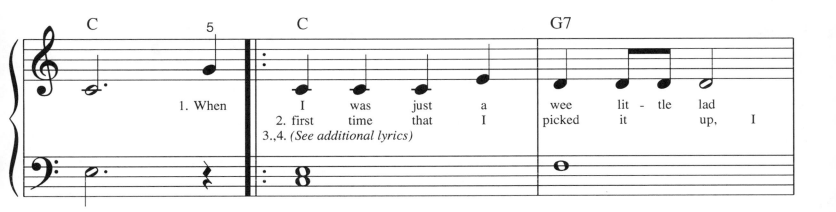

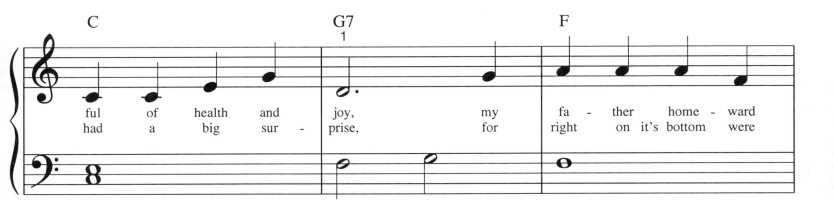

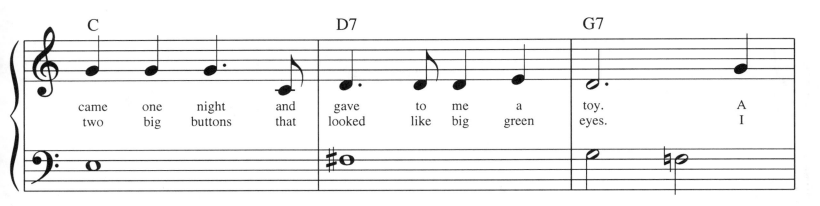

138

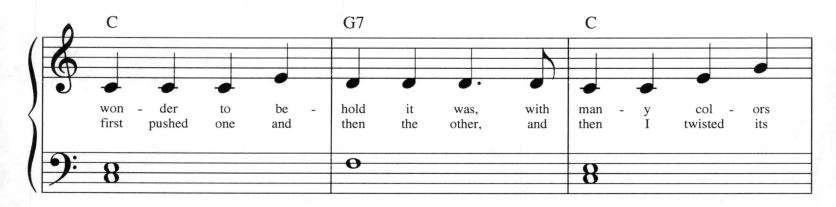

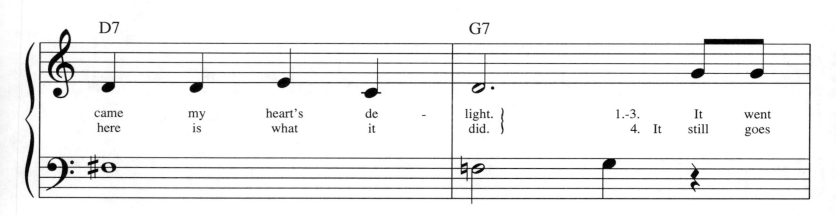

Chorus

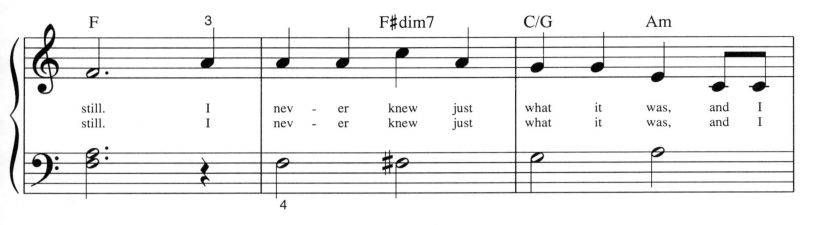

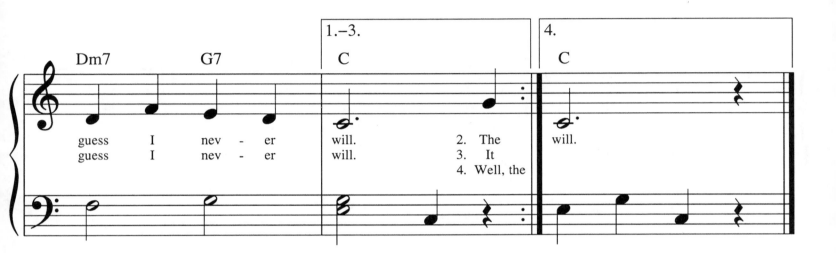

Additional Lyrics

3. It first marched left and then marched right,
   And then marched under a chair.
   And when I looked where it had gone,
   It wasn't even there!
   I started to sob and my daddy laughed,
   For he knew that I would find
   When I turned around my marvelous toy
   Chuggin' from behind.

   It went... *(Chorus)*

4. Well, the years have gone by too quickly, it seems,
   And I have my own little boy,
   And yesterday I gave to him
   My marv'lous little toy.
   His eyes nearly popped right out of his head,
   And he gave a squeal of glee.
   Neither one of us knows just what it is,
   But he loves it just like me.

   It still goes... *(Chorus)*

MICHAEL
(Row The Boat Ashore)

Traditional Folksong

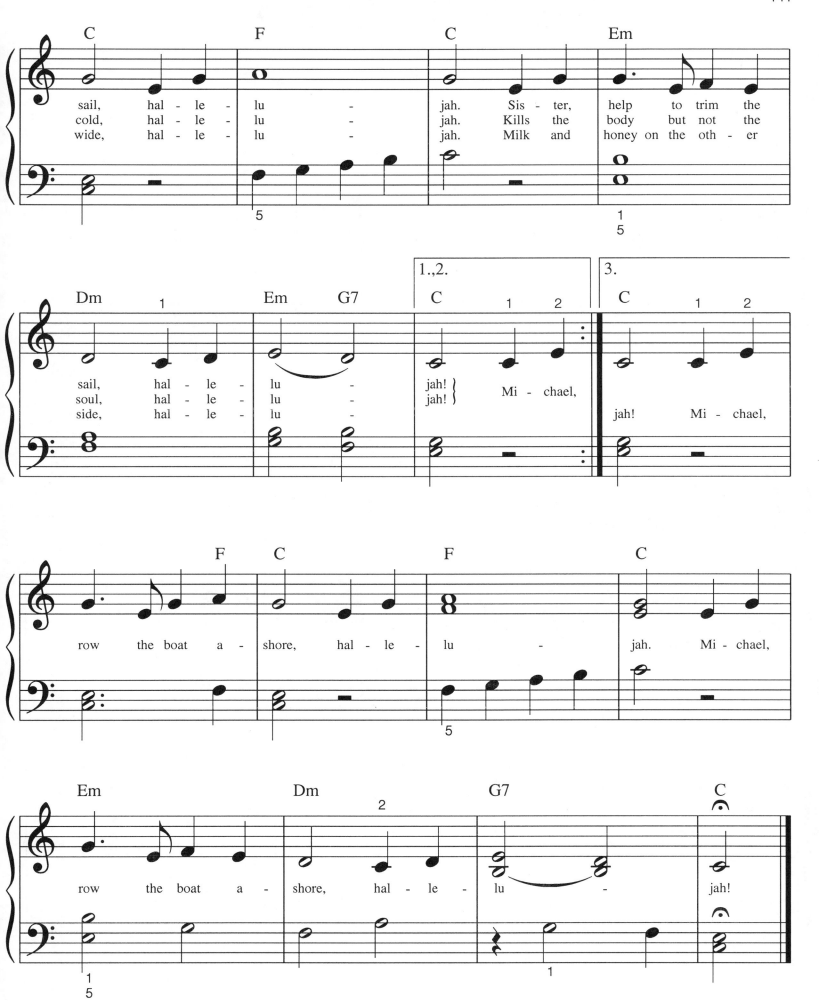

THE MUFFIN MAN

Traditional

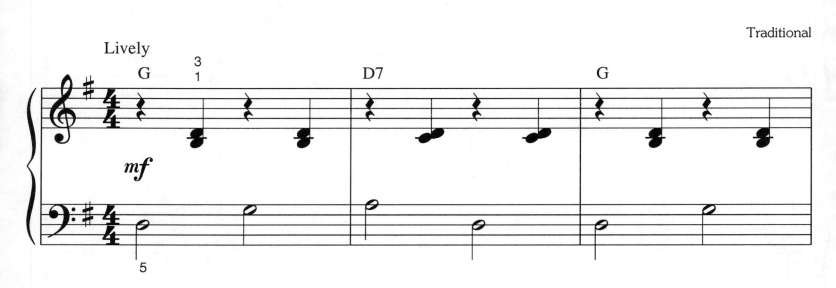

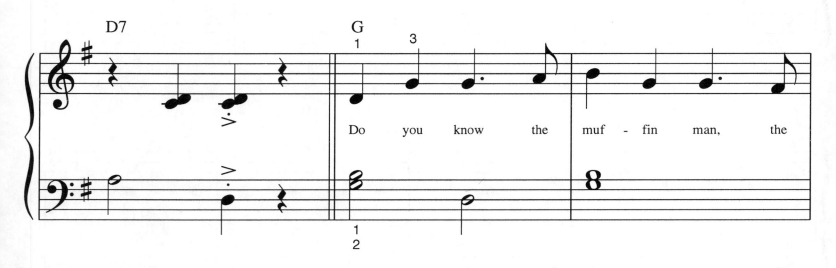

Do you know the muf - fin man, the

muf - fin man, the muf - fin man? Do you know the

MY BONNIE LIES OVER THE OCEAN

Flowing and spirited

Traditional

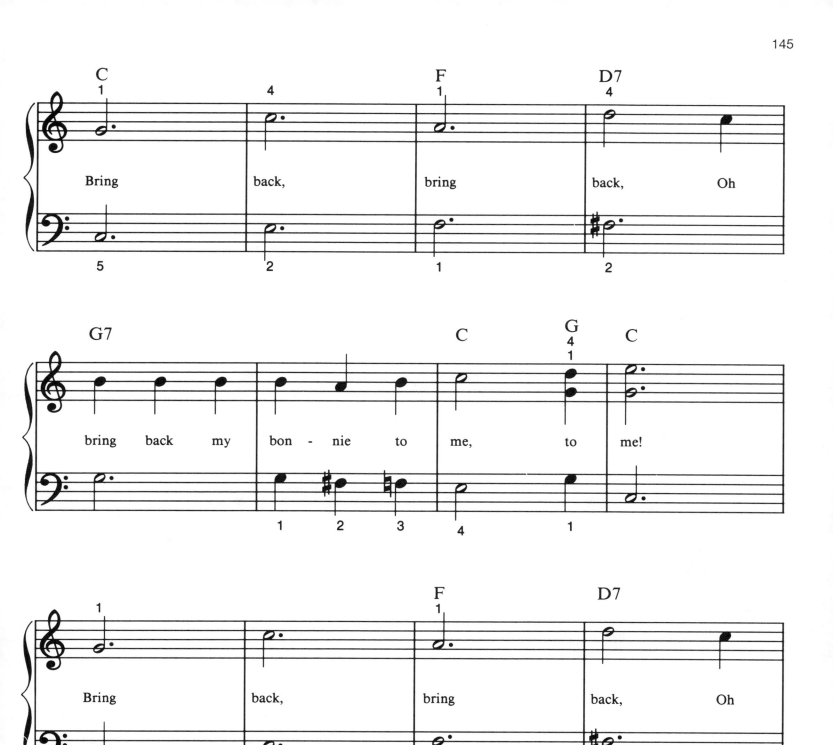
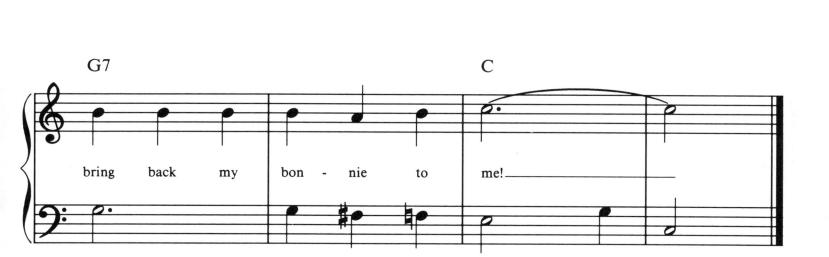

MARY HAD A LITTLE LAMB

Words by SARAH JOSEPHA HALE
Music is Traditional

OVER THE RIVER AND THROUGH THE WOODS

Traditional

ON THE GOOD SHIP LOLLIPOP

from BRIGHT EYES

Words and Music by SIDNEY CLARE
and RICHARD A. WHITING

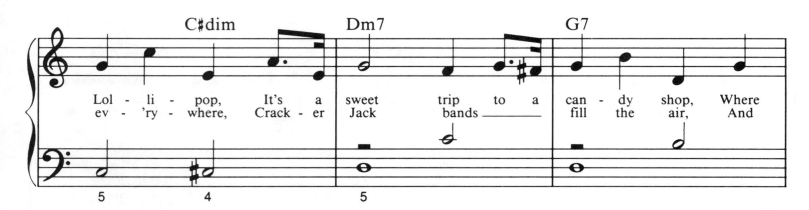

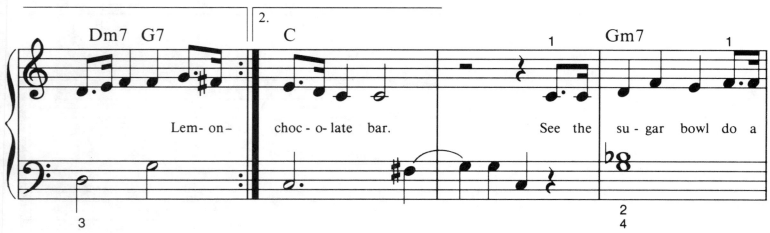

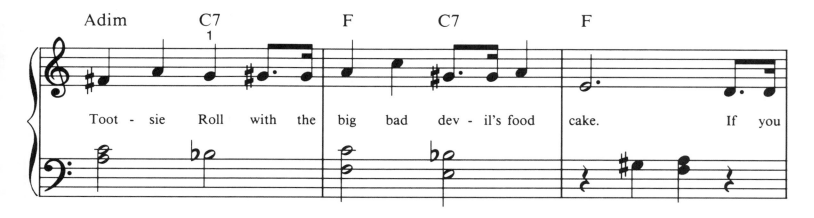

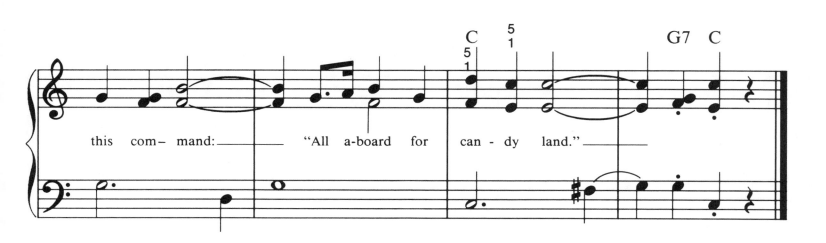

THE PAW PAW PATCH

Traditional

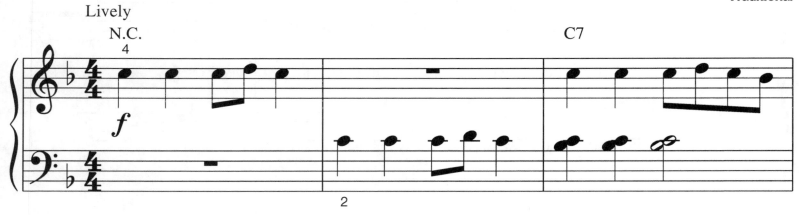

Where, oh, where is dear lit - tle Su - zy?

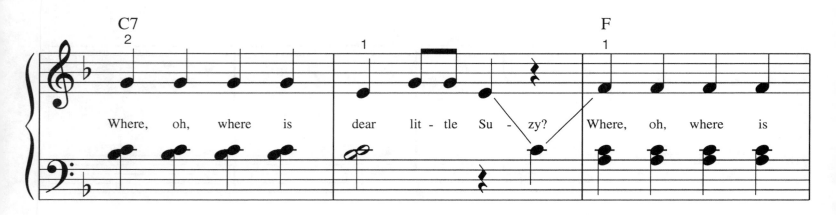

Where, oh, where is dear lit - tle Su - zy? Where, oh, where is

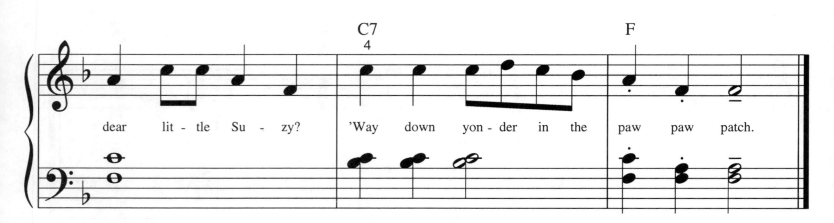

dear lit - tle Su - zy? 'Way down yon - der in the paw paw patch.

PEOPLE IN YOUR NEIGHBORHOOD

from the Television Series SESAME STREET

Words and Music by
JEFF MOSS

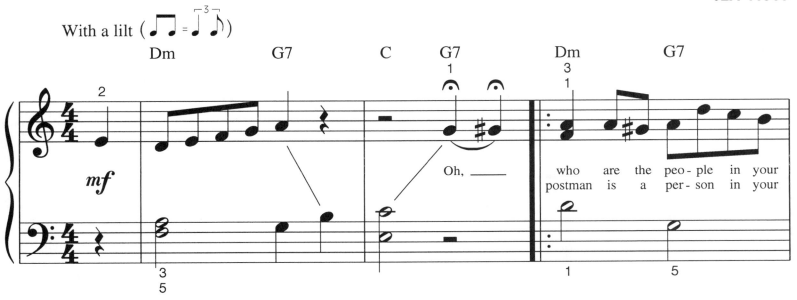

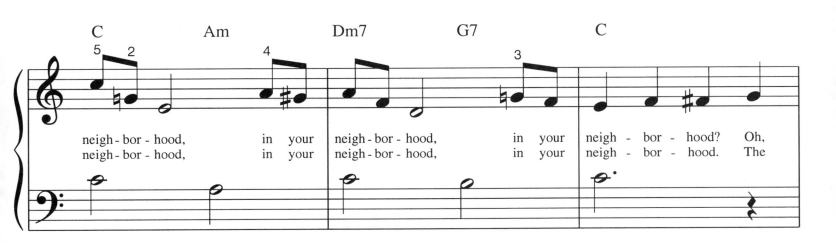

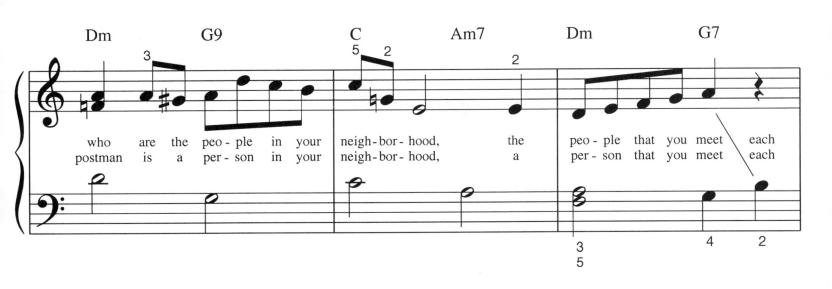

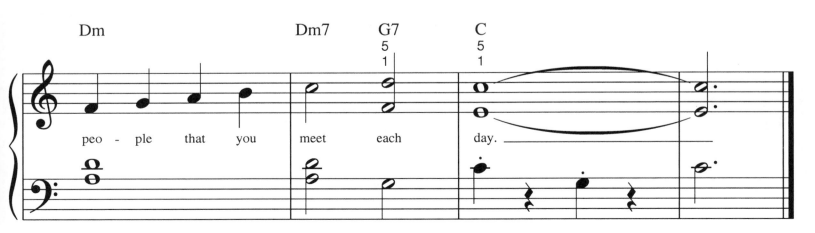

POLLY PUT THE KETTLE ON

Traditional

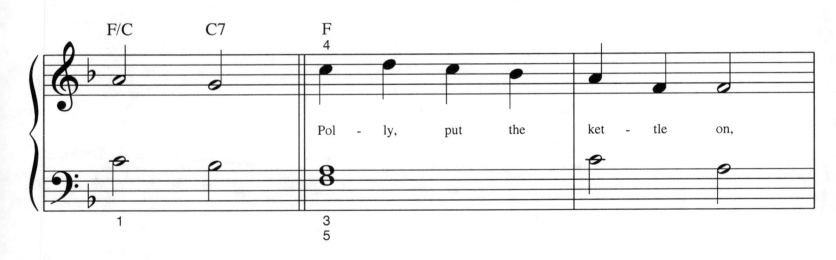

Pol - ly, put the ket - tle on,

Pol - ly, put the ket - tle on, Pol - ly, put the

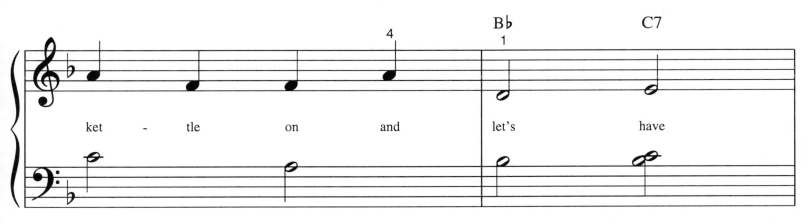

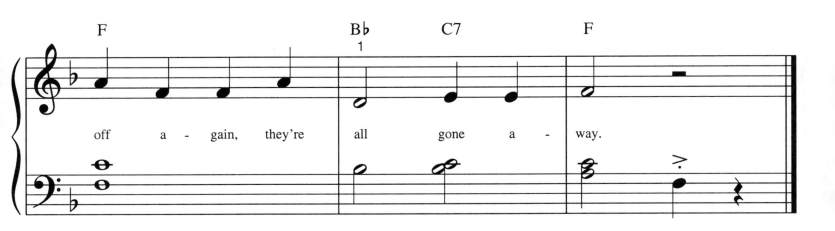

PUFF THE MAGIC DRAGON

Words by LEONARD LIPTON
Music by PETER YARROW

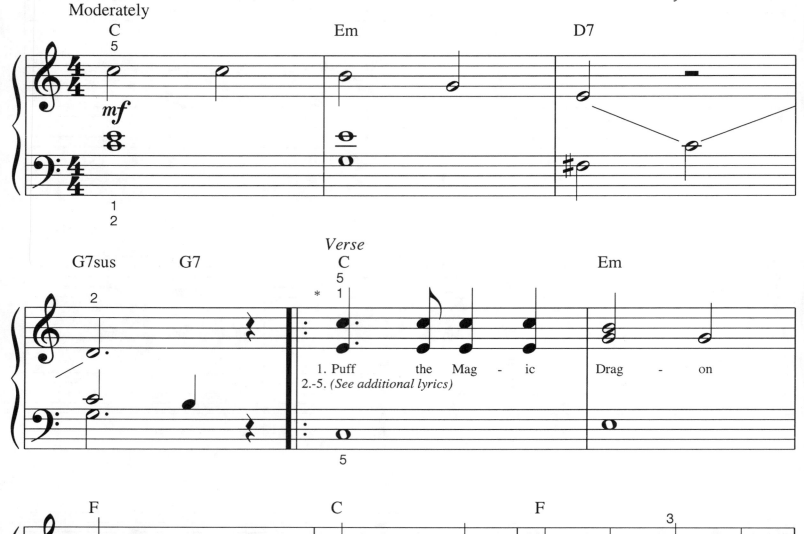

1. Puff the Mag - ic Drag - on
2.-5. *(See additional lyrics)*

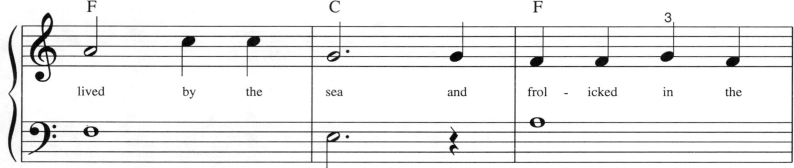

lived by the sea and frol - icked in the

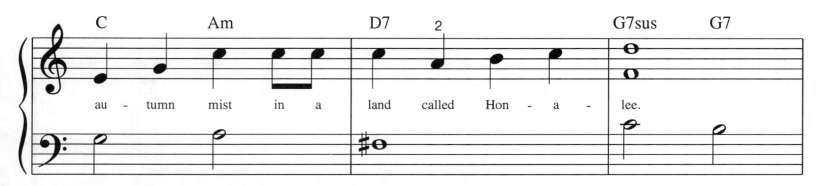

au - tumn mist in a land called Hon - a - lee.

After Verse 4, skip the Chorus and play Verse 5. Then play Chorus with last ending.

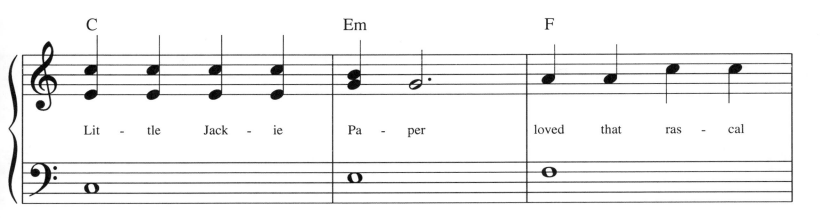

Lit - tle Jack - ie Pa - per loved that ras - cal

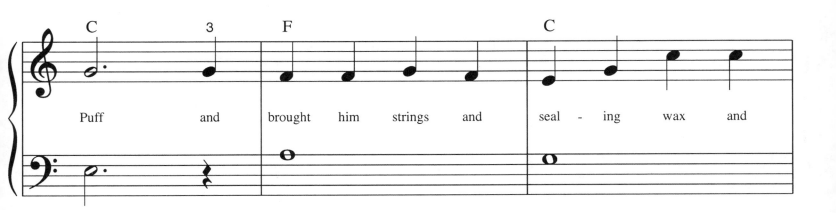

Puff and brought him strings and seal - ing wax and

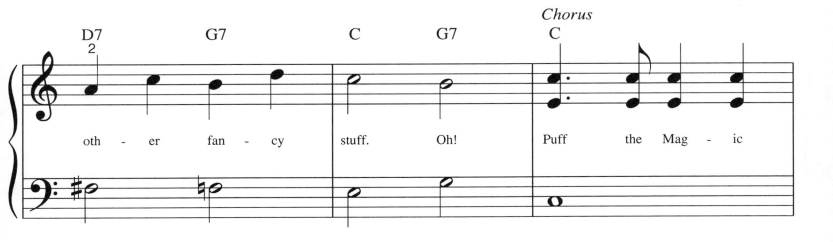

Chorus

oth - er fan - cy stuff. Oh! Puff the Mag - ic

Drag - on lived by the sea and

158

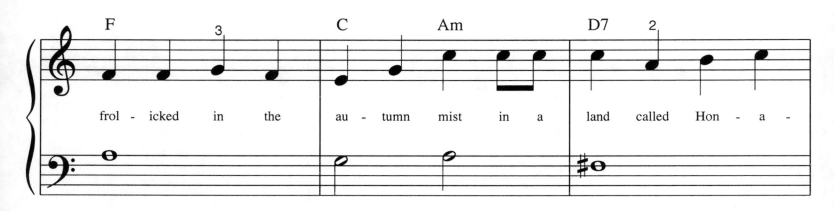

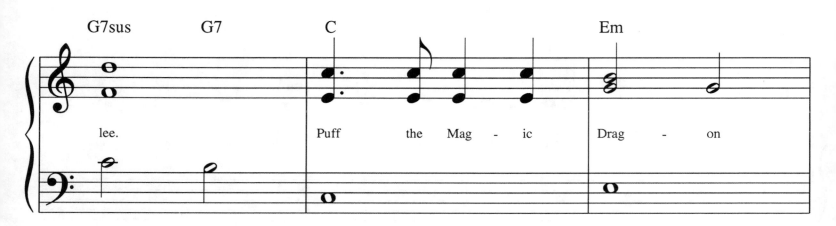

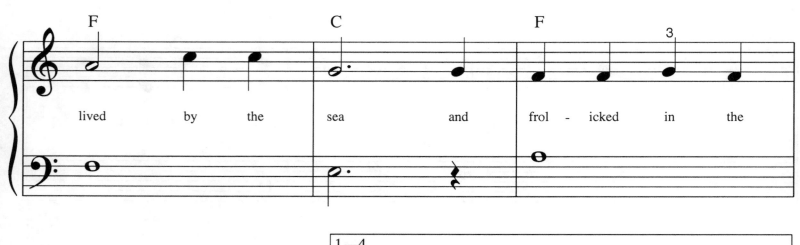

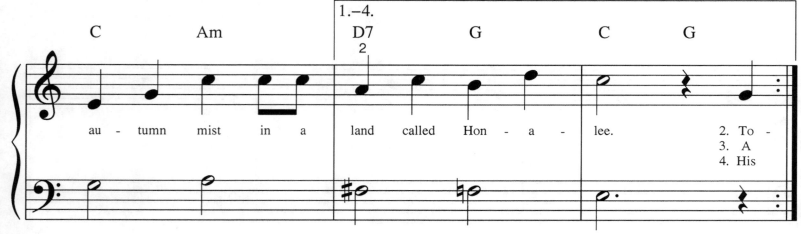

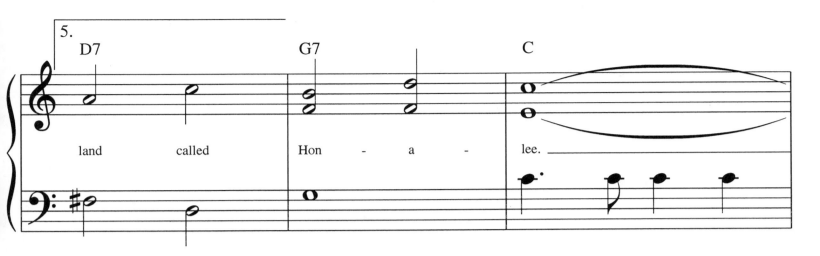

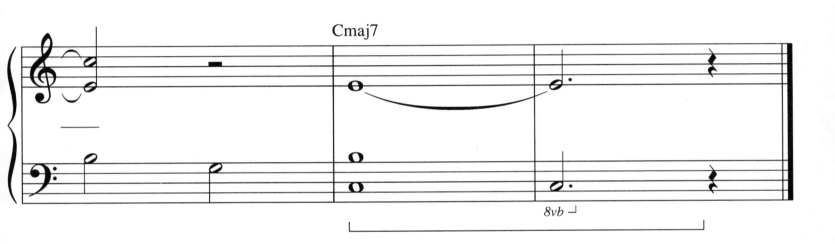

Additional Lyrics

2. Together they would travel on a boat with billowed sail.
   Jackie kept a lookout perched on Puff's gigantic tail.
   Noble kings and princes would bow whene'er they came.
   Pirate ships would low'r their flag when Puff roared out his name. Oh! *(Chorus)*

3. A dragon lives forever, but not so little boys.
   Painted wings and giant rings make way for other toys.
   One gray night it happened, Jackie Paper came no more,
   And Puff that mighty dragon, he ceased his fearless roar. Oh! *(Chorus)*

4. His head was bent in sorrow, green tears fell like rain.
   Puff no longer went to play along the Cherry Lane.
   Without his lifelong friend, Puff could not be brave,
   So Puff that mighty dragon sadly slipped into his cave.

*THE RETURN OF PUFF

5. Puff the Magic Dragon danced down the Cherry Lane.
   He came upon a little girl, Julie Maple was her name.
   She'd heard that Puff had gone away, but that can never be.
   So together they went sailing to the land called Honalee. *(Chorus)*

RUBBER DUCKIE
from the Television Series SESAME STREET

Words and Music by
JEFF MOSS

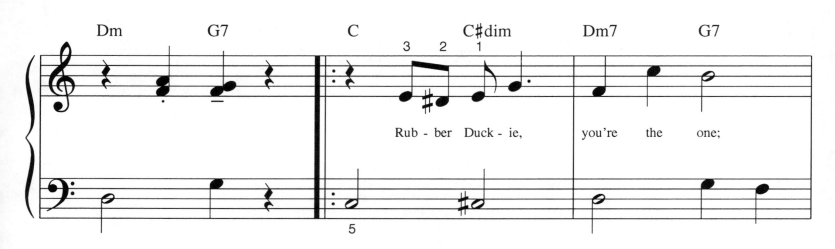

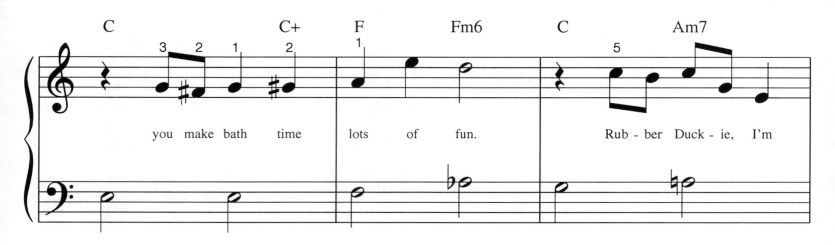

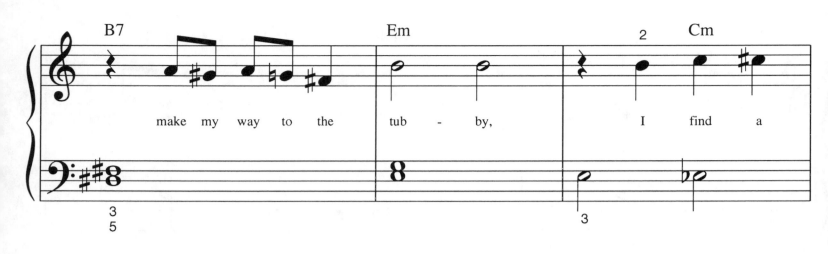

make my way to the tub - by, I find a

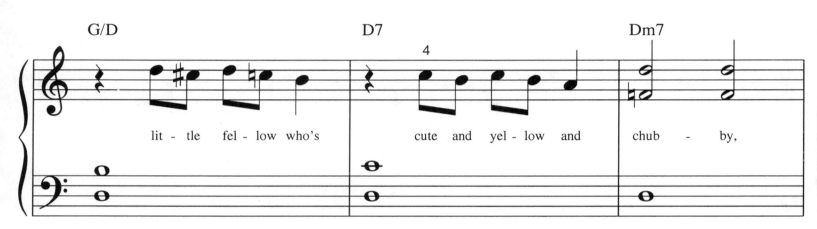

lit - tle fel - low who's cute and yel - low and chub - by,

Rub - a - dub - dub - by. Rub - ber Duck - ie, you're so fine,

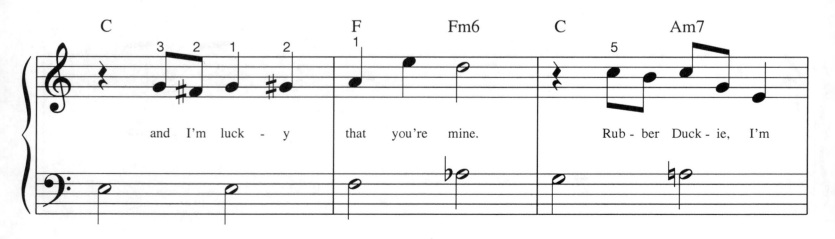

and I'm luck - y that you're mine. Rub - ber Duck - ie, I'm

SAILING, SAILING

Words and Music by
GODFREY MARKS

SING
from SESAME STREET

Words and Music by
JOE RAPOSO

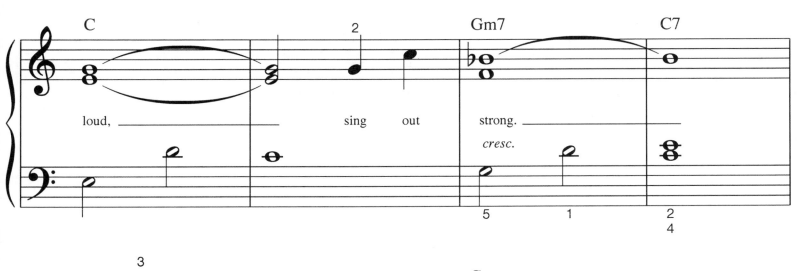

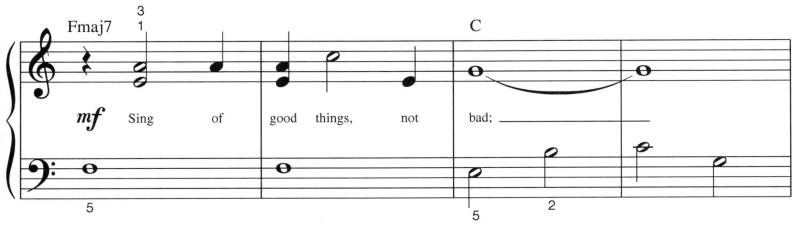

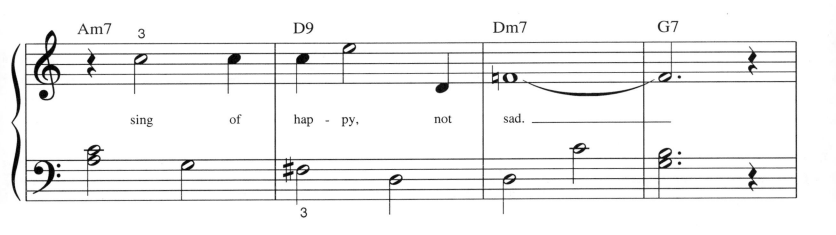

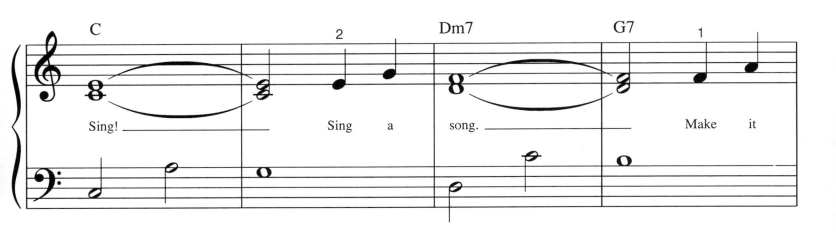

168

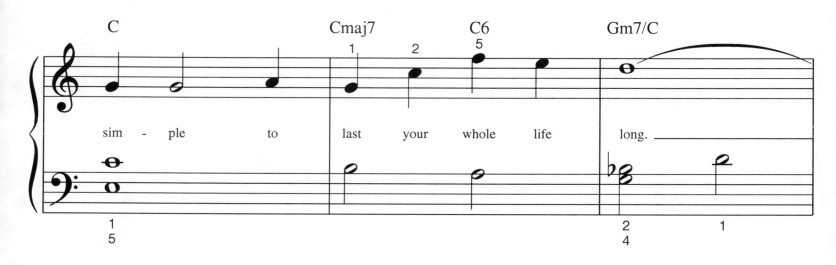

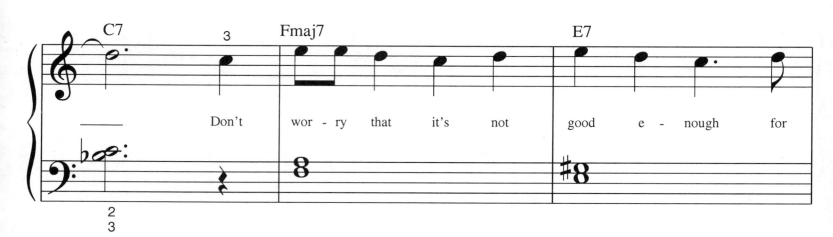

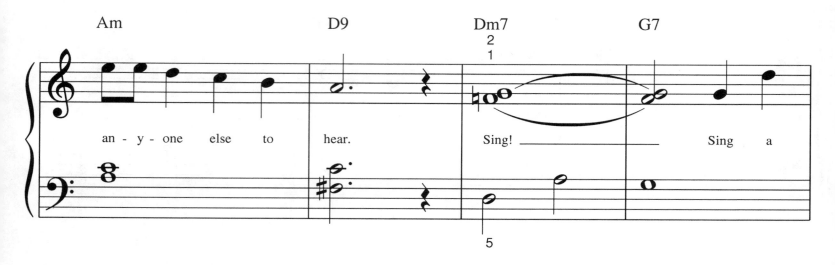

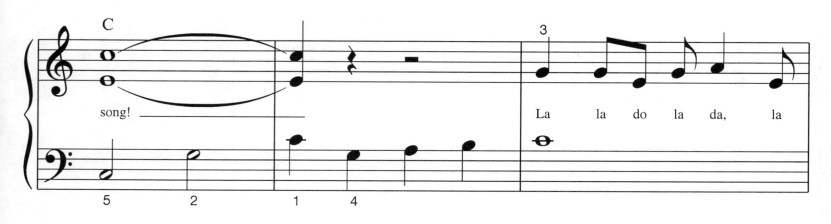

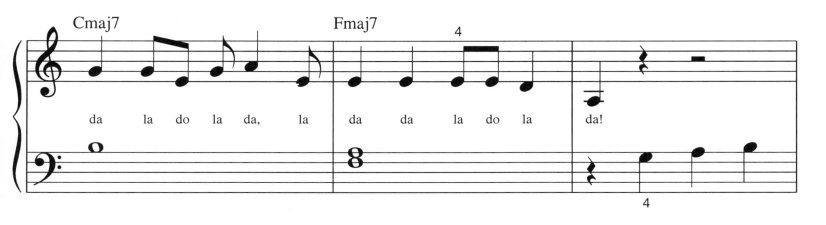

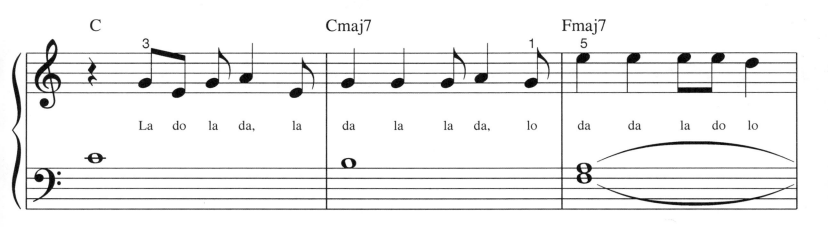

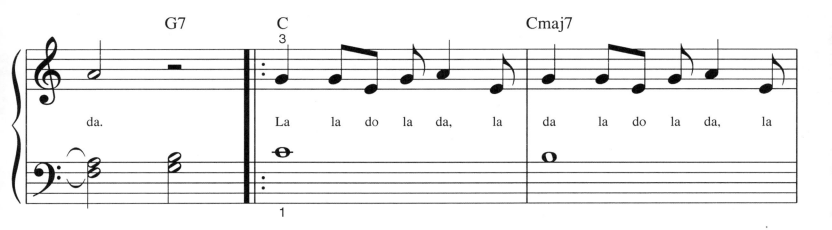

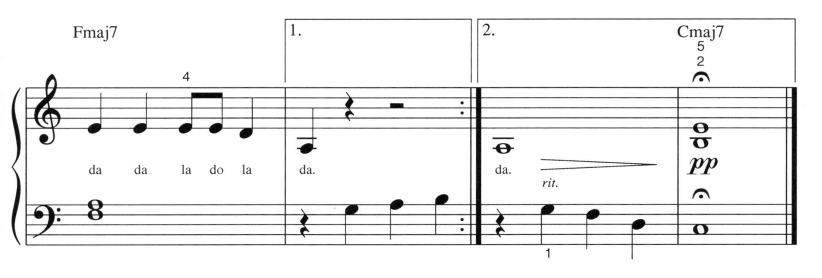

SING A SONG OF SIXPENCE

Traditional

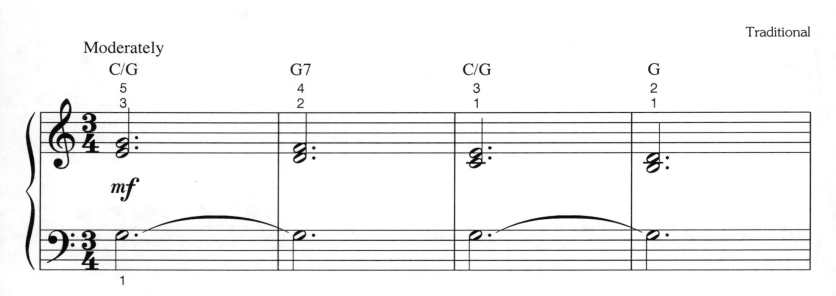

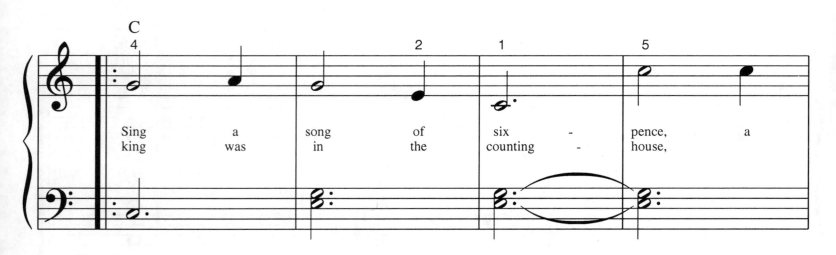

Sing a song of six - pence, a
king was in the counting - house,

171

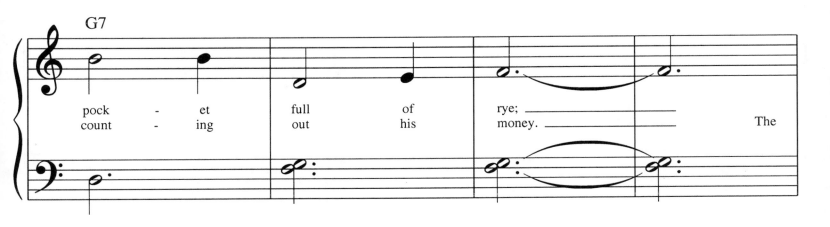

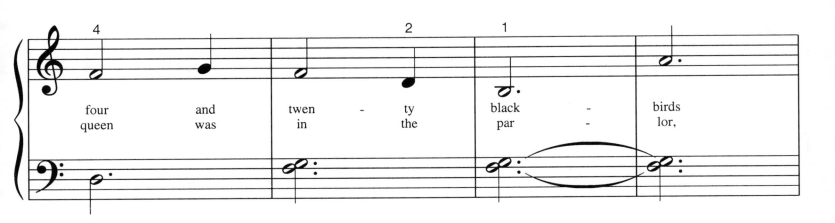

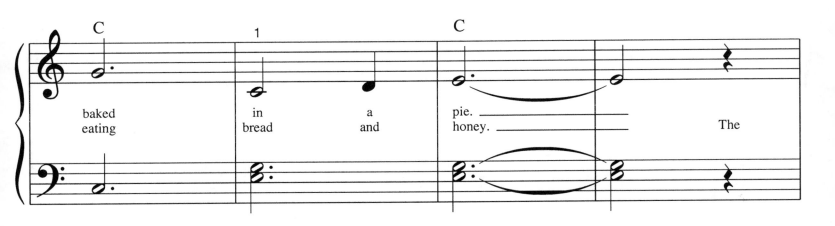

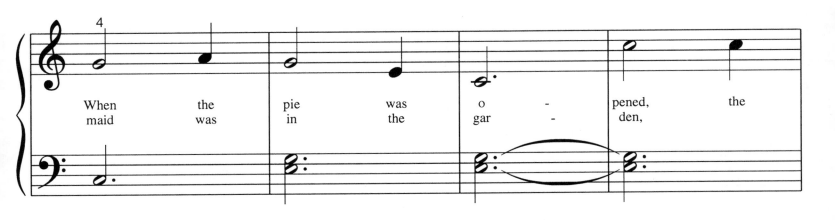

172

A SPOONFUL OF SUGAR

from Walt Disney's MARY POPPINS

Words and Music by RICHARD M. SHERMAN
and ROBERT B. SHERMAN

Moderately

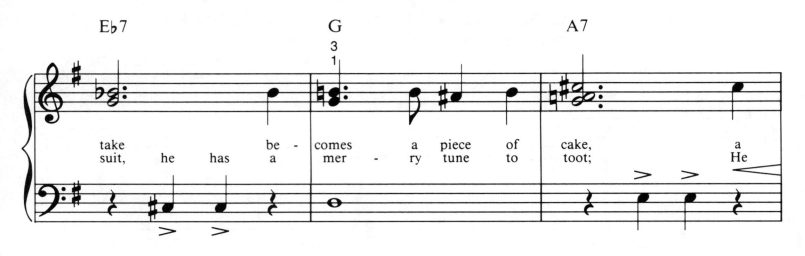

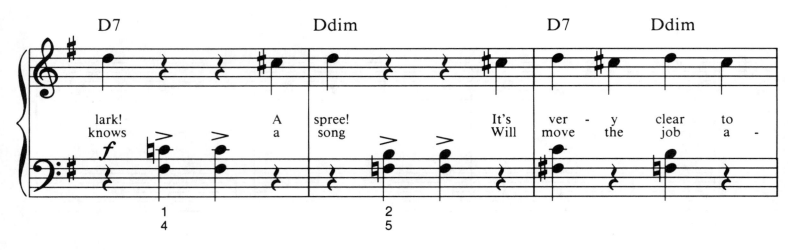

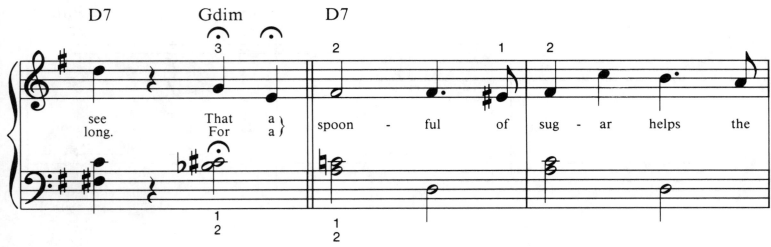

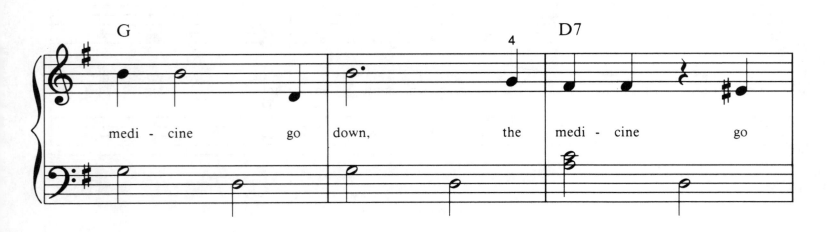

8va lower

SWEET BETSY FROM PIKE

Traditional

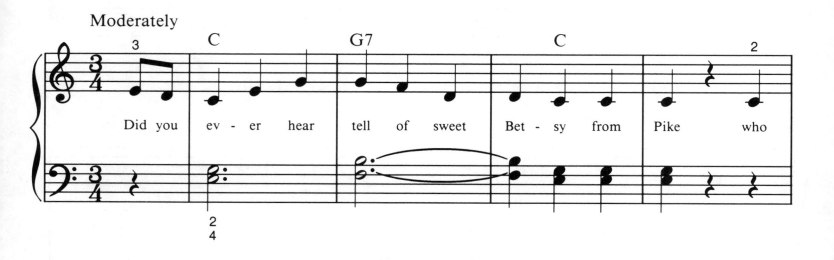

Moderately

Did you ev - er hear tell of sweet Bet - sy from Pike who

crossed the wide prai - rie with her lov - er, Ike With

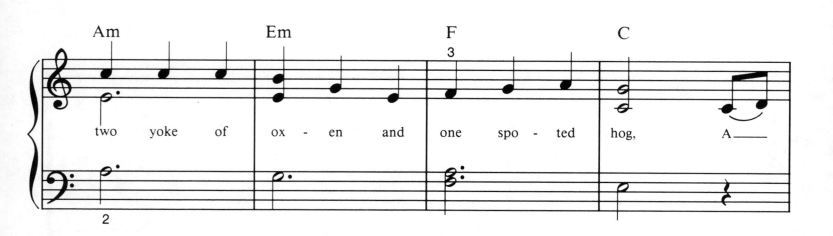

two yoke of ox - en and one spot - ted hog, A

177

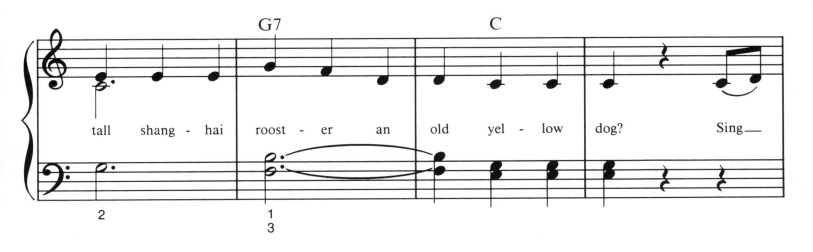

tall   shang - hai   roost - er   an   old   yel - low   dog?   Sing—

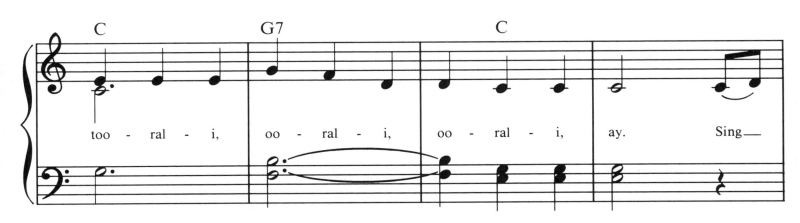

too - ral - i,   oo - ral - i,   oo - ral - i,   ay.   Sing—

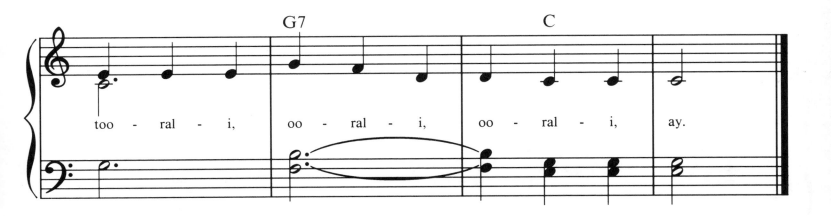

too - ral - i,   oo - ral - i,   oo - ral - i,   ay.

Additional Words

One evening quite early they camped on the Platte,
'Twas near by the road on a green shady flat;
Where Betsy, quite tired, lay down to repose,
While with wonder Ike gazed on his Pike County rose.

TAKE ME OUT TO THE BALL GAME

Words by JACK NORWORTH
Music by ALBERT von TILZER

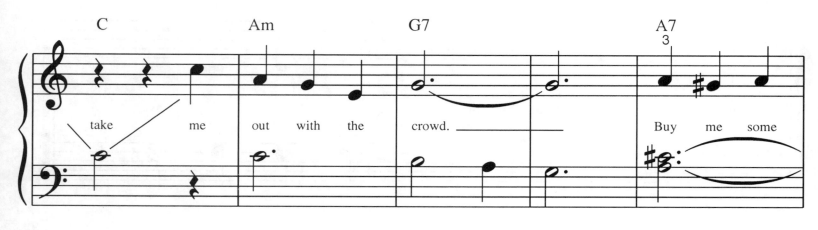

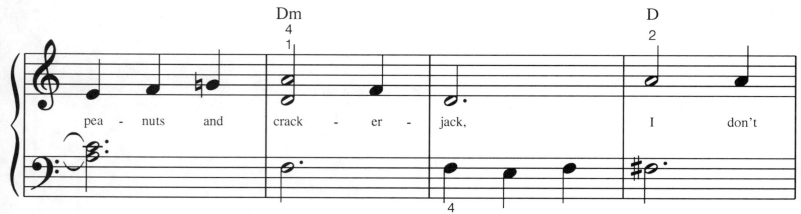

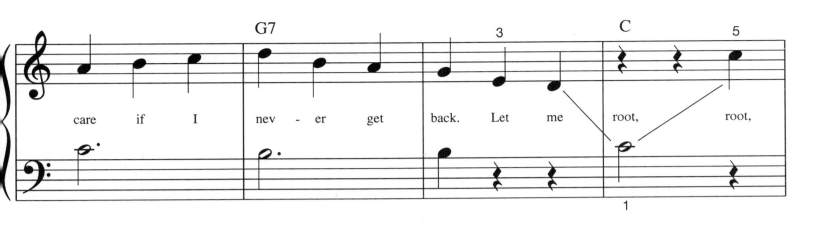

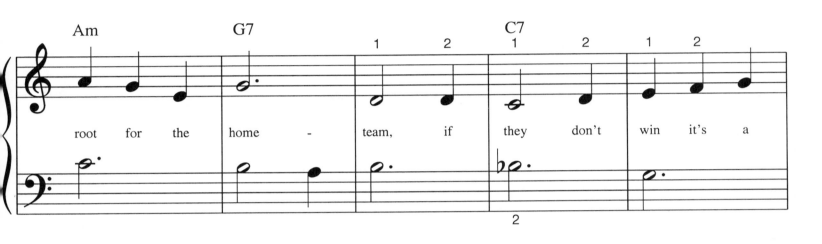

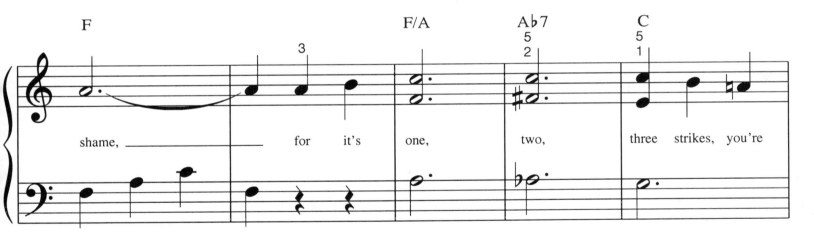

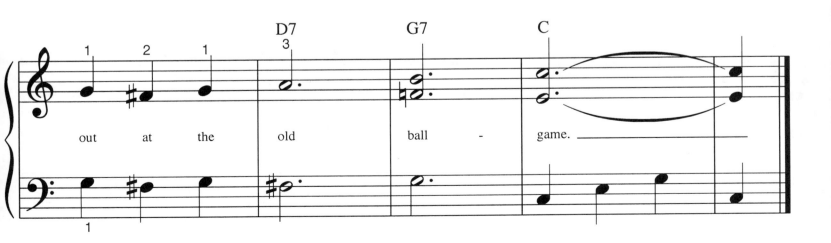

THERE'S A HOLE IN THE BOTTOM OF THE SEA

Traditional

Moderately

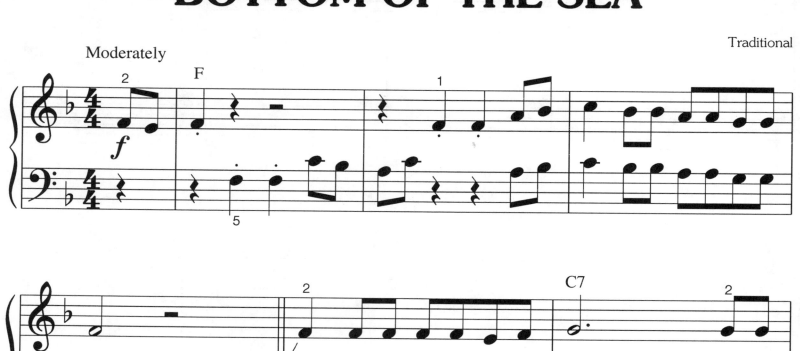

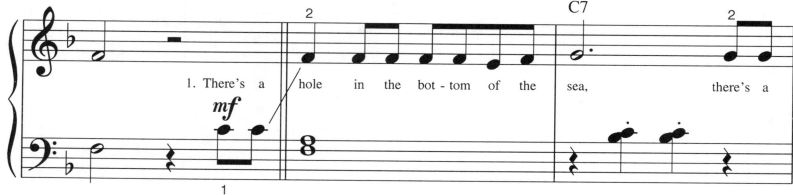

1. There's a hole in the bot-tom of the sea, there's a

hole in the bot-tom of the sea. There's a hole, there's a

A little faster
with each verse

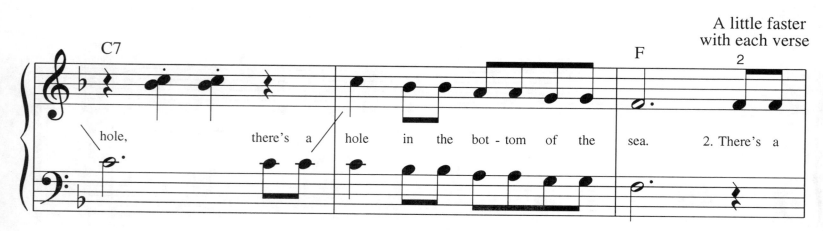

hole, there's a hole in the bot-tom of the sea. 2. There's a

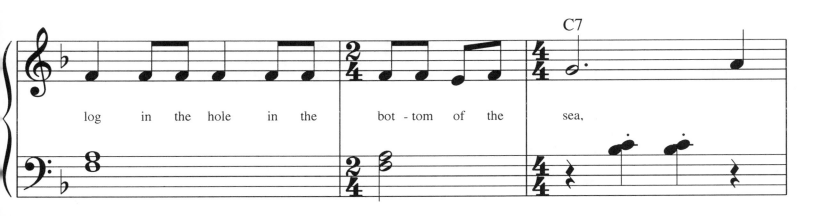

log in the hole in the bot - tom of the sea,

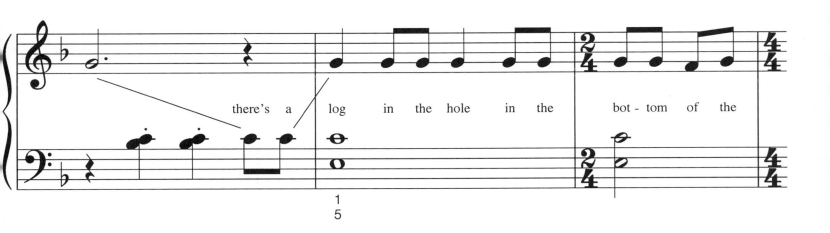

there's a log in the hole in the bot - tom of the

1
5

sea. There's a log, there's a

log, there's a log in the hole in the bot - tom of the

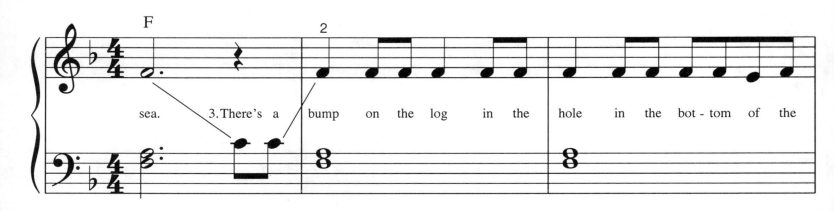

sea. 3. There's a bump on the log in the hole in the bot- tom of the

sea, there's a bump on the log in the

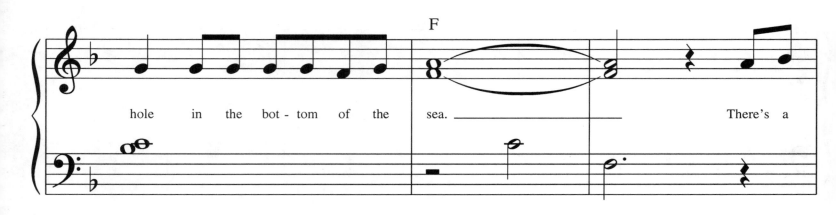

hole in the bot- tom of the sea. _____ There's a

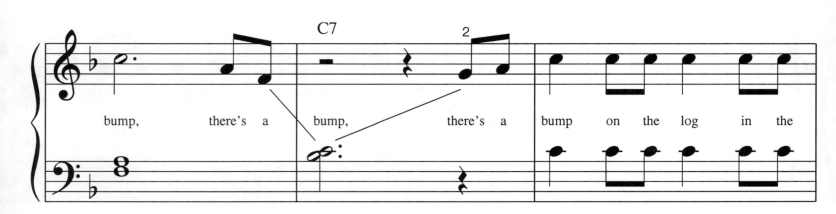

bump, there's a bump, there's a bump on the log in the

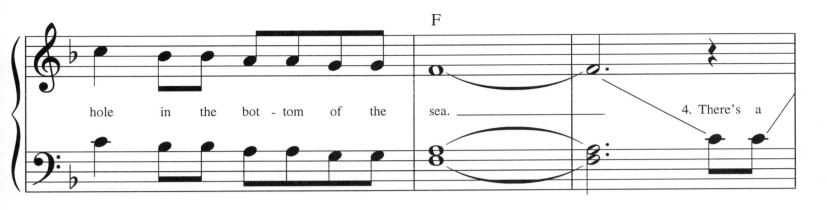

hole in the bot - tom of the sea. _____ 4. There's a

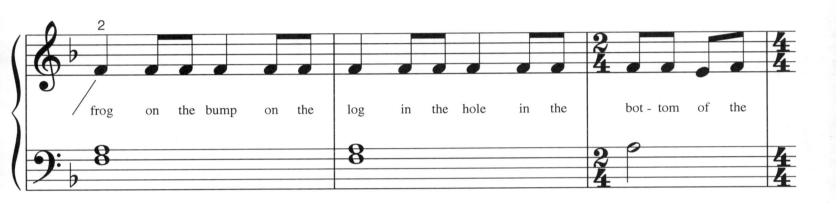

frog on the bump on the log in the hole in the bot - tom of the

C7

sea, _____ there's a frog on the bump on the

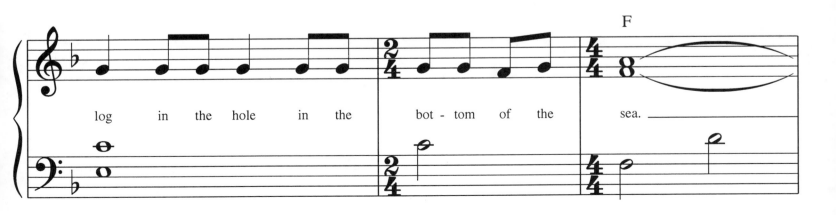

F

log in the hole in the bot - tom of the sea. _____

184

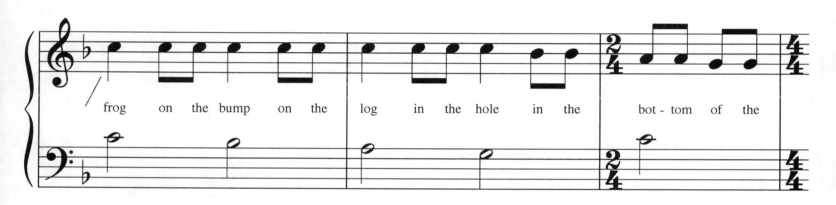

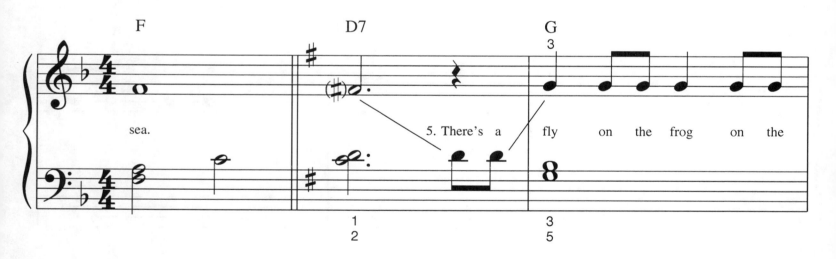

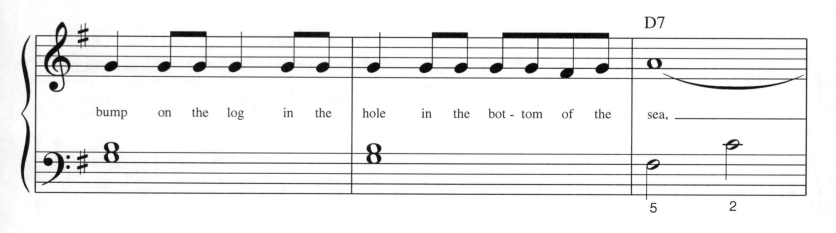

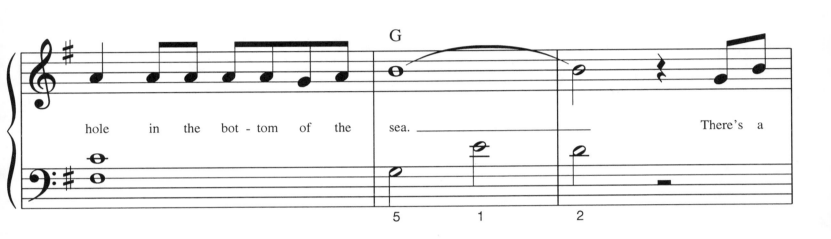

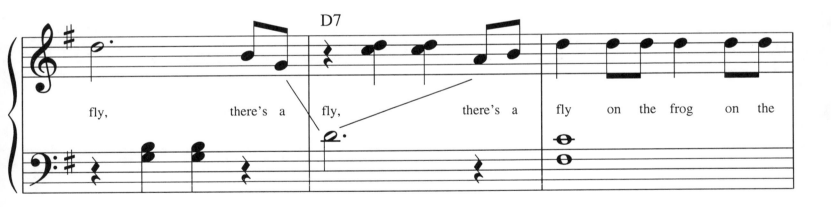

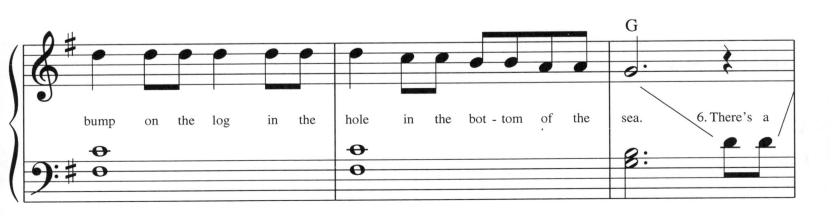

wing on the fly on the frog on the bump on the log in the hole in the

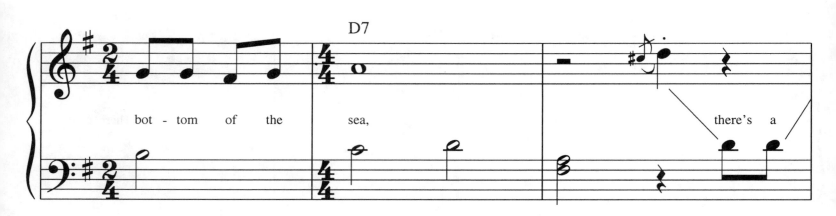

bot - tom of the sea, there's a

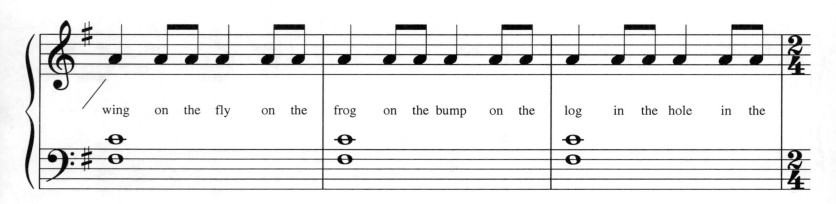

wing on the fly on the frog on the bump on the log in the hole in the

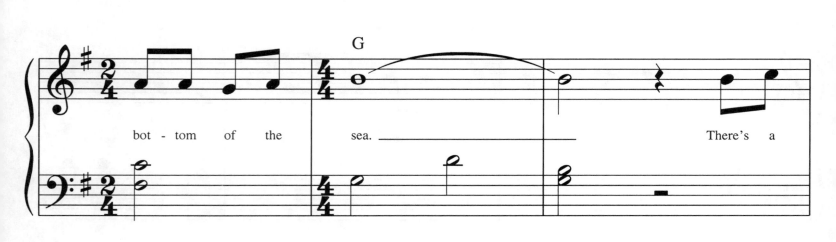

bot - tom of the sea. There's a

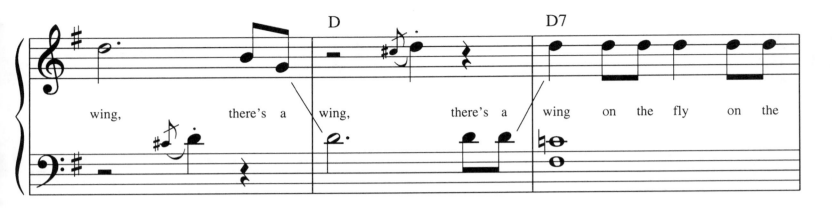

wing, there's a wing, there's a wing on the fly on the

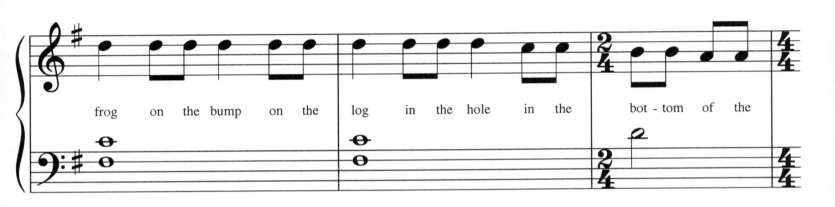

frog on the bump on the log in the hole in the bot - tom of the

sea. _____ 7. There's a flea on the wing on the

fly on the frog on the bump on the log in the hole in the bot - tom of the

188

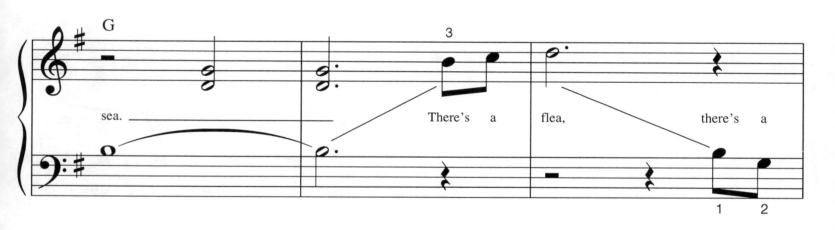

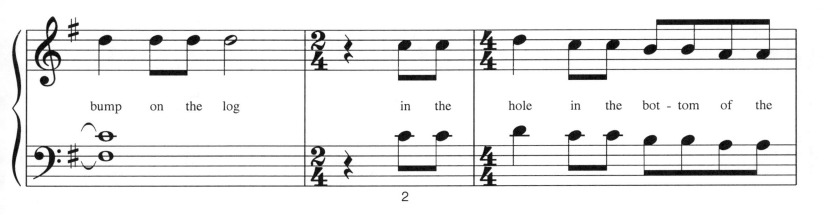

bump on the log in the hole in the bot - tom of the

2

sea. 8. There's an eye on the flea on the wing of the fly on the

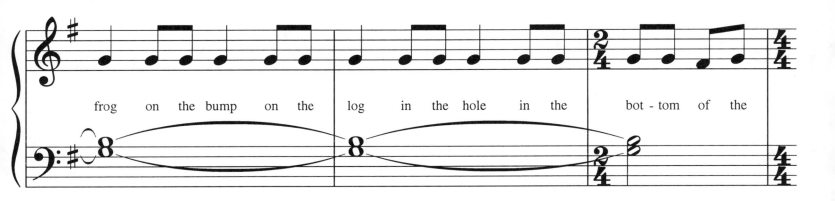

frog on the bump on the log in the hole in the bot - tom of the

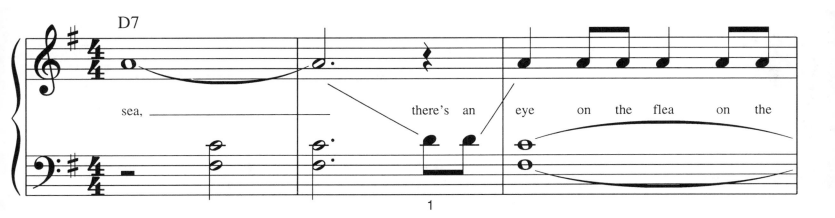

sea, there's an eye on the flea on the

1

190

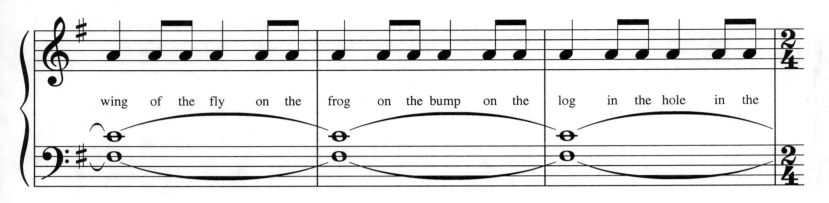

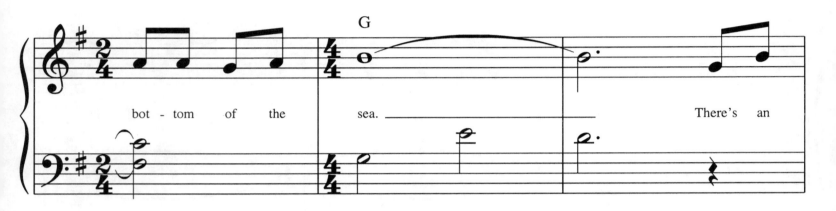

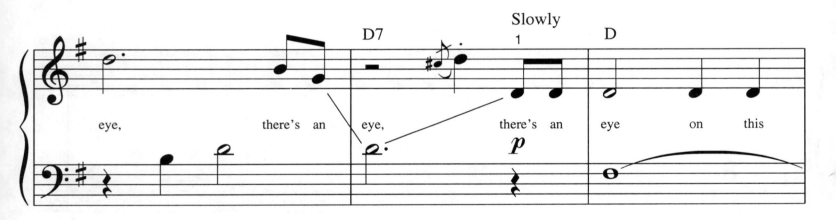

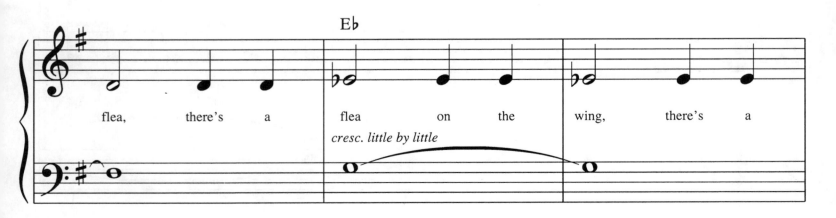

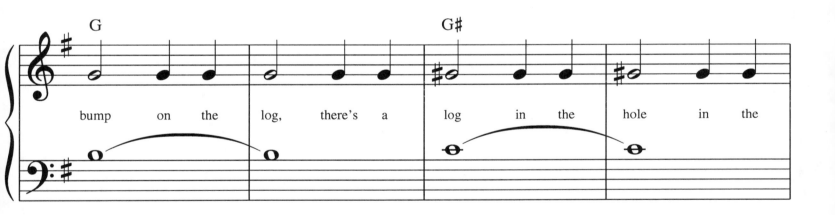

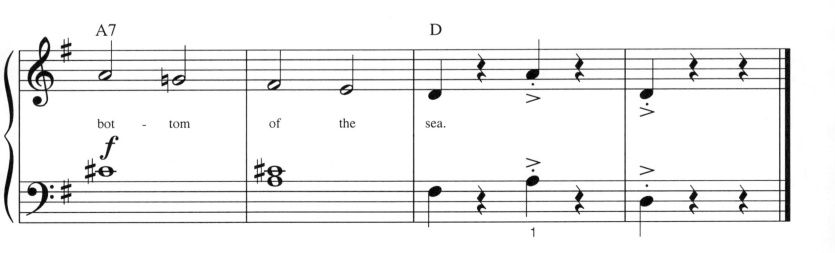

THIS TRAIN

Traditional

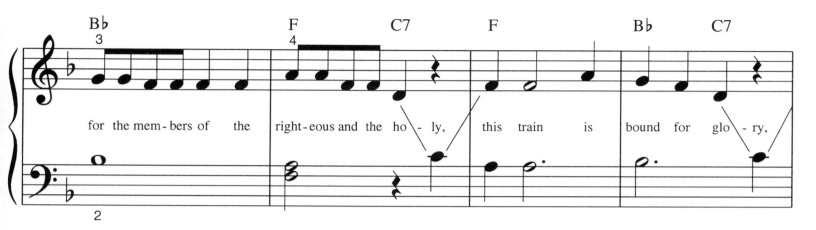

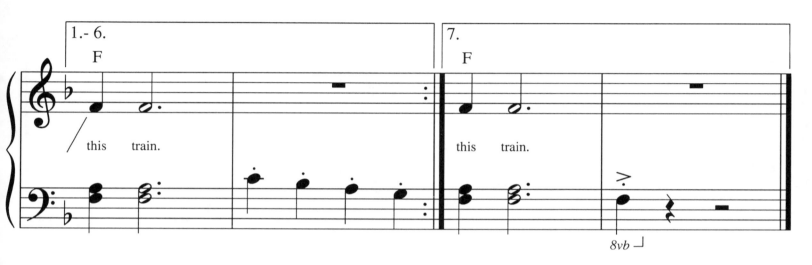

Additional Lyrics

2. This train takes no deceivers,
   This train.
   This train takes no deceivers,
   This train.
   This train takes no deceivers,
   Takes no hypocrites and non-believers,
   This train is bound for glory, this train!

3. This train don't carry no fakers,
   This train.
   This train don't carry no fakers,
   This train.
   Won't stop for cheatin' fakers,
   Idle gossips and trouble makers,
   This train is bound for glory, this train!

4. This train don't carry meddlers,
   This train.
   This train don't carry meddlers,
   This train.
   Won't stop for mischievous meddlers,
   Gives no tickets to narcotic peddlers,
   This train is bound for glory, this train!

4. This train don't carry sinners,
   This train.
   This train don't carry sinners,
   This train.
   This train don't carry sinners,
   No prevaricating tall-tale spinners,
   This train is bound for glory, this train!

5. So if you wnat to ride on
       this train,
   Look who you'll sit beside
       on this train:
   Folks who their ways have mended,
   Folks who live the way the Lord intended,
   This train is bound for glory, this train!

6. And if you qualify
       this train,
   You'll need no pass to buy
       for this train.
   Be kind, be fair and patient,
   Show your neighbor no discrimination,
   This train is bound for glory, this train!

THERE'S A HOLE IN THE BUCKET

Traditional

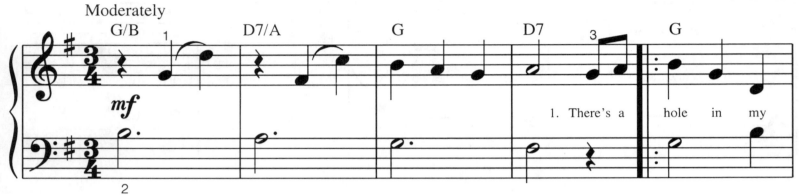

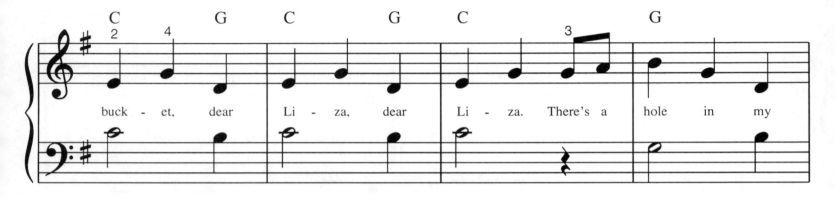

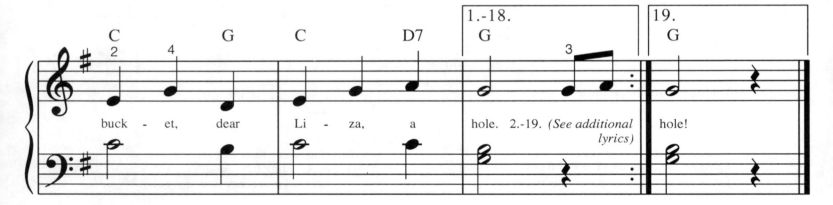

Additional Lyrics

2. Well, fix it, dear Henry, etc.
3. With what shall I fix it, dear Liza, etc.
4. With a straw, dear Henry, etc.
5. But the straw is too long, dear Liza, etc.
6. Then cut it, dear Henry, etc.
7. With what shall I cut it, dear Liza, etc.
8. With a knife, dear Henry, etc.
9. But the knife is too dull, dear Liza, etc.
10. Then sharpen it, dear Henry, etc.
11. With what shall I sharpen it, dear Liza, etc.
12. With a stone, dear Henry, etc.
13. But the stone is too dry, dear Liza, etc.
14. Then wet it, dear Henry, etc.
15. With what shall I wet it, dear Liza, etc.
16. With water, dear Henry, etc.
17. In what shall I carry it, dear Liza, etc.
18. In a bucket, dear Henry, etc.
19. There's a hole in my bucket, dear Liza, etc.

THE UNBIRTHDAY SONG
from Walt Disney's ALICE IN WONDERLAND

Words and Music by MACK DAVID,
AL HOFFMAN and JERRY LIVINGSTON

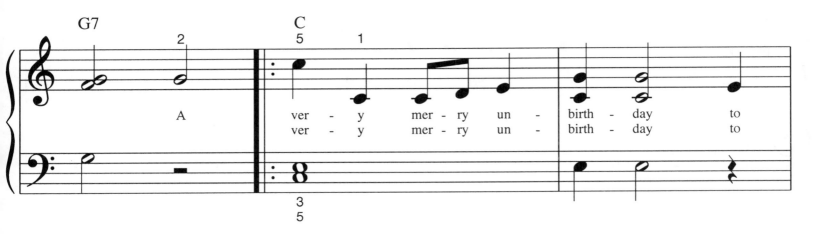

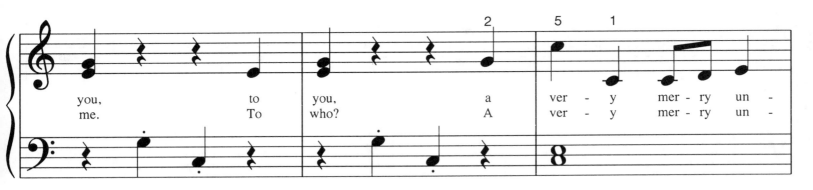

great   to drink to   some - one and I   guess that you will
all   con - grat - u -   late me with a   pres - ent, I a -

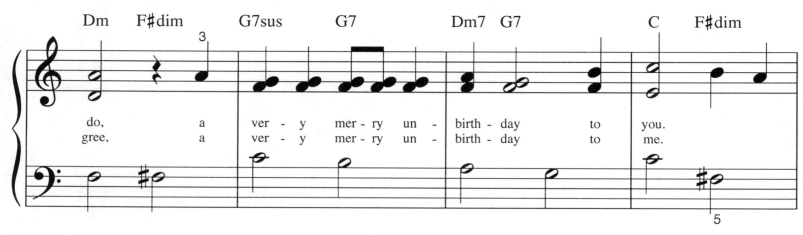

do,   a   ver - y mer - ry un - birth - day to   you.
gree,   a   ver - y mer - ry un - birth - day to   me.

A   ver - y mer - ry un - birth - day to us,   to
A   ver - y mer - ry un - birth - day to all,   to

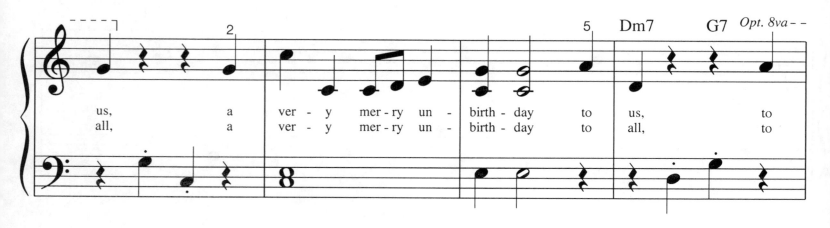

us,   a   ver - y mer - ry un - birth - day to us,   to
all,   a   ver - y mer - ry un - birth - day to all,   to

UNDER THE SEA
from Walt Disney's THE LITTLE MERMAID

Lyrics by HOWARD ASHMAN
Music by ALAN MENKEN

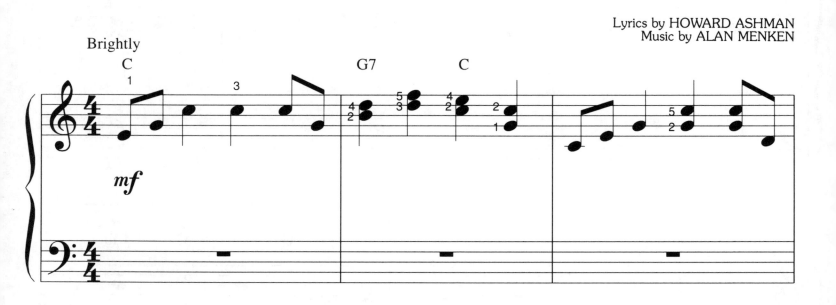

The sea-weed is al - ways green - er
Down here all the fish is hap - py

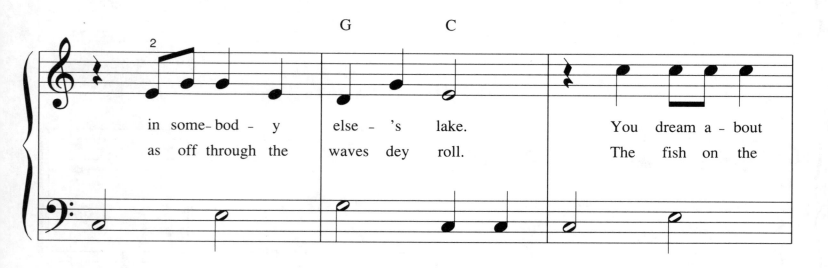

in some-bod - y else - 's lake. You dream a - bout
as off through the waves dey roll. The fish on the

202

Oh, that blow – fish blow.

Un – der the

207

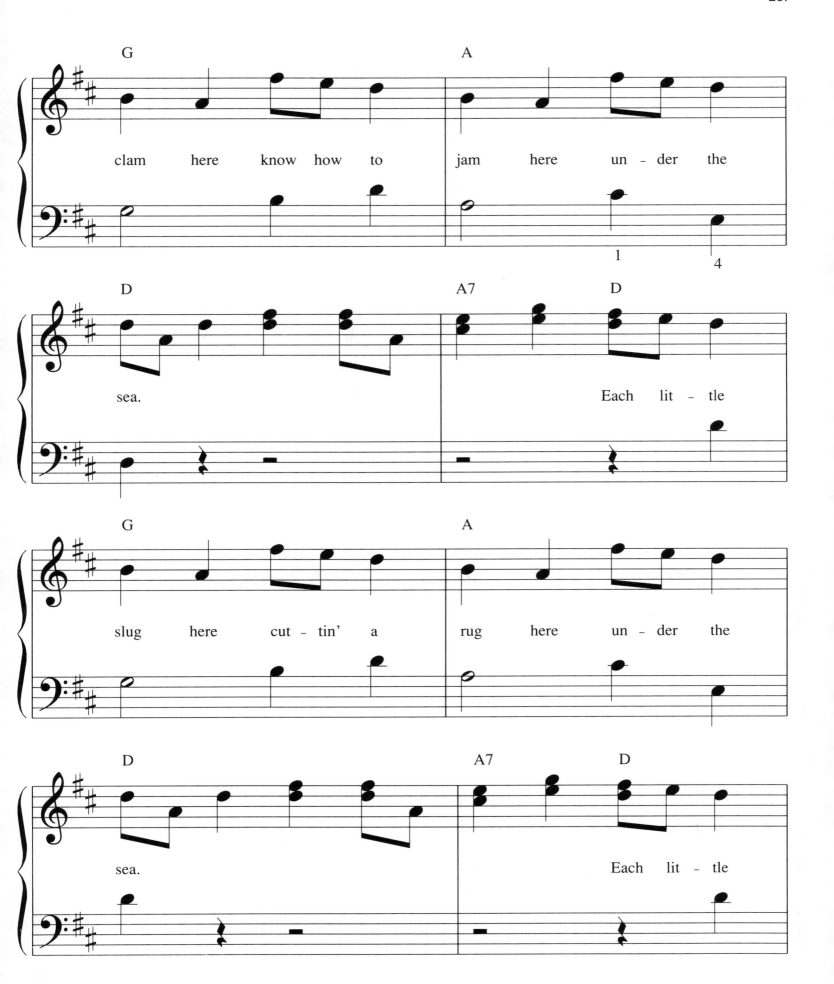

WHEN JOHNNY COMES MARCHING HOME

Words and Music by
PATRICK SARSFIELD GILMORE (LOUIS LAMBERT)

WHEN THE SAINTS GO MARCHING IN

Words by KATHERINE E. PURVIS
Music by JAMES M. BLACK

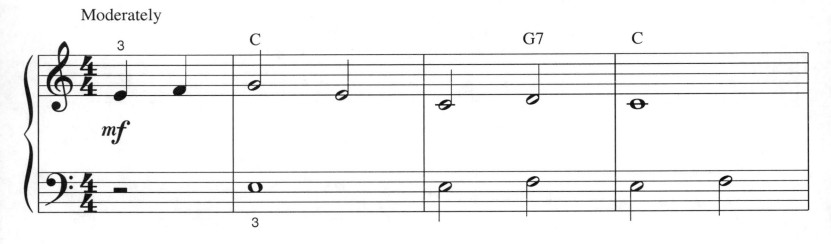

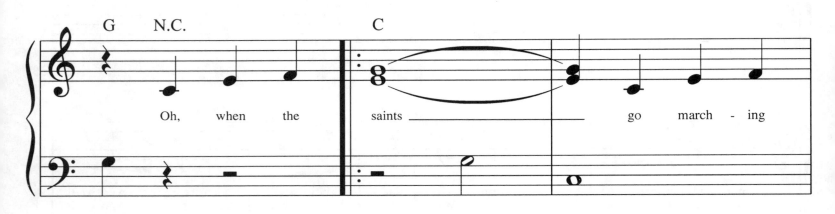

Oh, when the saints _____ go march - ing

in, _____ oh, when the saints go

WHO'S AFRAID OF THE BIG BAD WOLF

from Walt Disney's THREE LITTLE PIGS

Words and Music by FRANK CHURCHILL
Additional Lyric by ANN RONELL

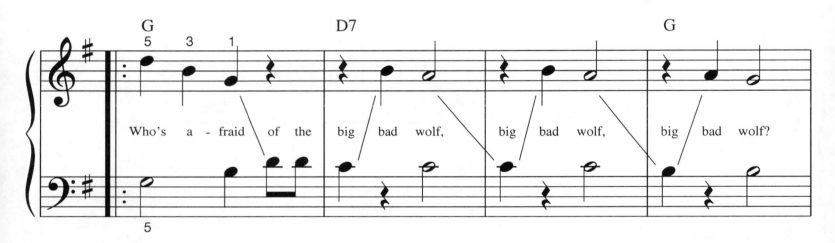

Who's a-fraid of the big bad wolf, big bad wolf, big bad wolf?

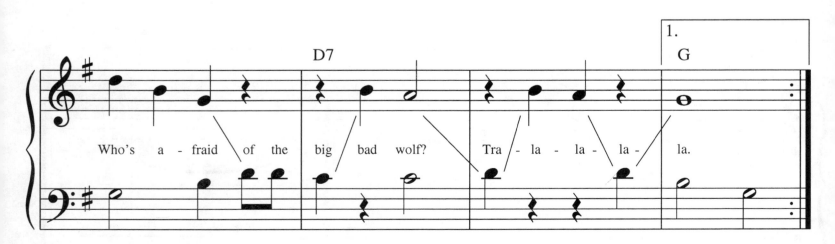

Who's a-fraid of the big bad wolf? Tra-la-la-la-la.

A WHOLE NEW WORLD
from Walt Disney's ALADDIN

Music by ALAN MENKEN
Lyrics by TIM RICE

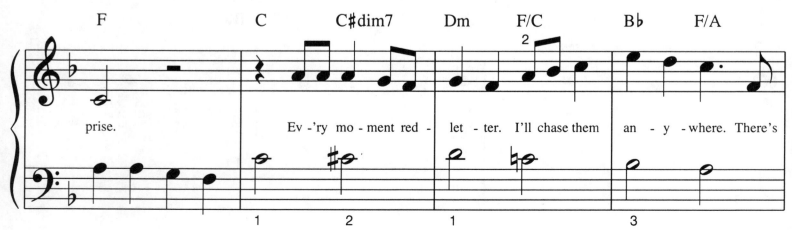

WON'T YOU BE MY NEIGHBOR?

(a/k/a It's A Beautiful Day In This Neighborhood)
from MISTER ROGERS' NEIGHBORHOOD

Words and Music by
FRED ROGERS

It's a

beau - ti - ful day in this neigh - bor - hood, a beau - ti - ful day for a neigh - bor. Would you
neigh - bor - ly day in this beau - ty - wood, a neigh - bor - ly day for a beau - ty. Would you

be / mine? Could you be / mine? It's a
be / mine? Could you be / mine?

be / mine? I have

al - ways want - ed to have a neigh - bor just like you! _ I've al - ways want - ed to live in a neigh - bor-

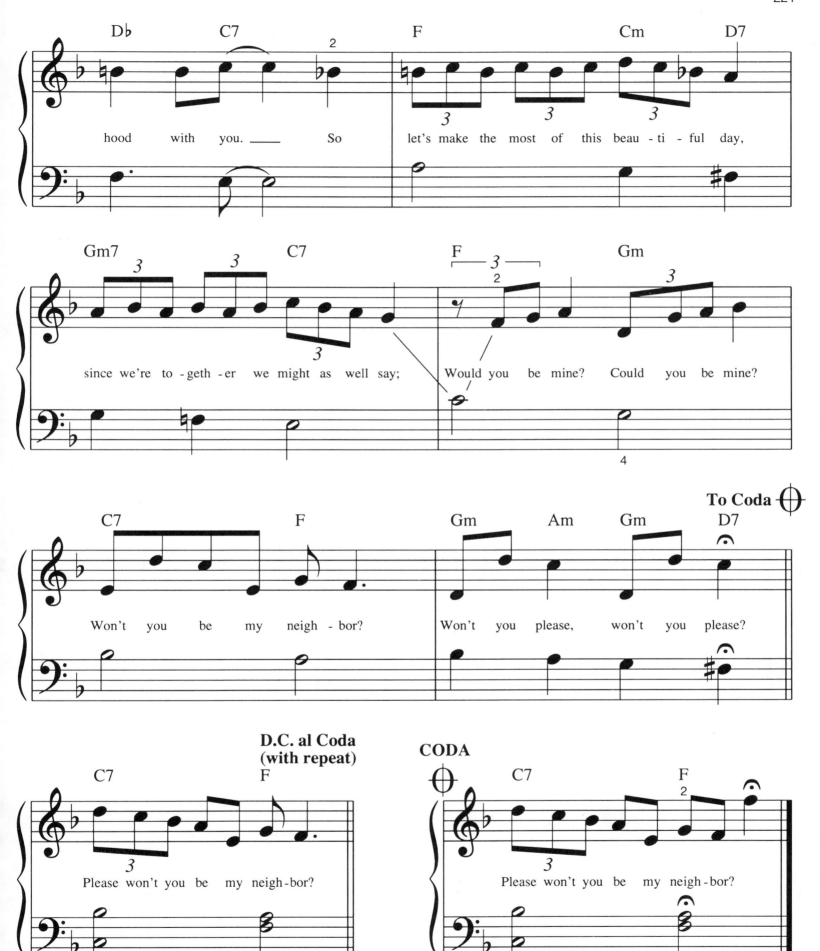

ZIP-A-DEE-DOO-DAH
from Walt Disney's SONG OF THE SOUTH

Words by RAY GILBERT
Music by ALLIE WRUBEL

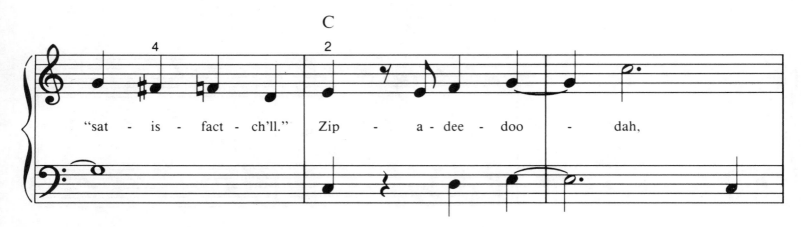

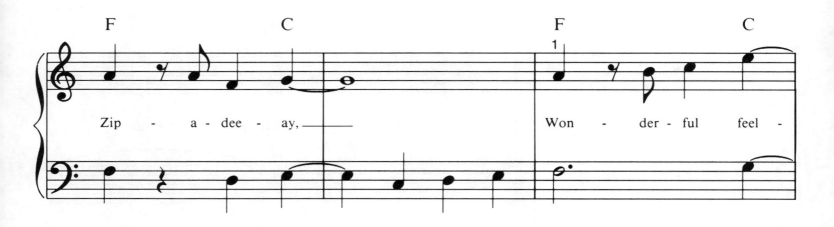

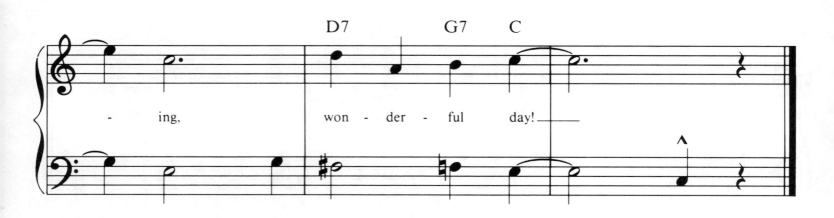